About the author...

Johnny Cashback is one of many pseudonyms that author Rob Mills goes by, with this particular one stemming from him never having any ready money and requesting it via card at the checkout – the Johnny part comes from his love of psychobilly rockers and the performer Johnny Cash. He is a self-proclaimed 'master of many and jack of none' having a wide and varied career as a writer, performer, teacher and glorified roadie.

A graduate in Education Studies as well as a lifetime member of the Millennium Fellowship, his accolades also include: CSV Yorkshire Trainee Journalist of the Year (1994), Zig Zag North Socapex Cabling Champion (1997) and Unsigned King of the Blaggers at the Reading Festival (1998), rivalling the signed Mathew Priest of the band Dodgy back in the day – the latter being his most treasured achievement.

He has travelled extensively, spent all of his money on instruments that he'll never learn to play and now lives in a tiny one bedroomed flat near Halifax, West Yorkshire – it's nice, but only a few of his showbiz friends ever come to visit.

Johnny would like to thank you for buying this book because as well as the money pit that comes with having children, his rent and utility payments are due next week…so cheers and tell your friends!

No part of this publication may be reproduced, distributed, or transmitted in any form or by any means, including photocopying, recording, or other electronic or mechanical methods, without the prior written permission of the publisher or author, except as permitted by copyright law and including the Berne Convention for the Protection of Literary and Artistic Works amended on 28th September 1979.

This publication is designed to provide accurate and authoritative information in regard to the subject matter covered. It is sold with the understanding that neither the author nor the publisher is engaged in rendering legal, investment, accounting or other professional services.

While the publisher and author have used their best efforts in preparing this book, they make no representations or warranties with respect to the accuracy or completeness of the contents of this book and specifically disclaim any implied warranties of merchantability or fitness for a particular purpose. No warranty may be created or extended by sales representatives or written sales materials.

The advice, opinions and strategies contained herein may not be suitable for your situation. You should consult with a professional where appropriate. Neither the publisher nor the author shall be liable for any loss of profit or any other commercial damages, including but not limited to special, incidental, consequential, personal or other damages.

Cover design: RPM Industries

Images sourced from:
www.freepik.comfree-photodoctor-s-hand-holding-stethoscope-closeup_15668927.htm
(front)

www.pixabay.comphotospills-medicine-health-medication-5246783
(back)

heart-rate-gaa517f4a1_1920
(spine)

First edition 2023
Copyright © 2023 by Rob Mills
All rights reserved.

ISBN: 9798395156815

*for Doodles –
you are my everything*

Life in The Valley

Preface	25
Hotel California	27
Screamager	31
Comfortably Numb	34
If It Makes You Happy	37
What I've Done	40
The Day I Tried Tried To Live	43
Who Knew?	46
Simple Man	48
Battery	52
Save Myself	56
The Lost Art Of Keeping A Secret	59
Disciple	64
Livin' On The Edge	66

Smoke 'Em	68
Jigsaw Puzzle	72
The Man Who Sold The World	75
Only Happy When It Rains	81
Orange Tree Roads	84
Bringin' On The Heartbreak	87
Sweet Soul Sister	92
State Of Love & Trust	97
The Drugs Don't Work	101
Wandering Star	106
Check My Brain	111
Chop Suey	115
Nearly Lost You	120
Heaven Knows I'm Miserable Now	123

Streets Of Philadelphia	125
Mr Jones	128
Ode To My Family	134
Big Gay Heart	146
Don't Believe A Word	149
Wanted Dead Or Alive	155
Wasted Years	159
Self Esteem	165
Low Self Opinion	171
Bullet With Butterfly Wings	177
Accidents Can Happen	180
Psycho Killer	183
Stand Up	189
Don't Let Me Be Misunderstood	194

Adam's Song	198
Don't Shit Where You Eat	201
Fisherman's Blues	204
Outside/Inside	207
Waking Up	211
Last Christmas	216
King Of The Whole Wide World	219
Lucille	224
Say A Little Prayer	230
Kids	234
Bleed American (Salt, Sweat, Sugar)	240
Caught In A Mosh	246
Bad Liver & A Broken Heart	249
Many Of Horror	251

Arlandria	257
What is Dysthymia (PDD)	271
Quotes	275
Guess The Lyrics Game	277
Discography	293
References	303
Roll Of Honour/Dishonour	337
Disclaimers	339

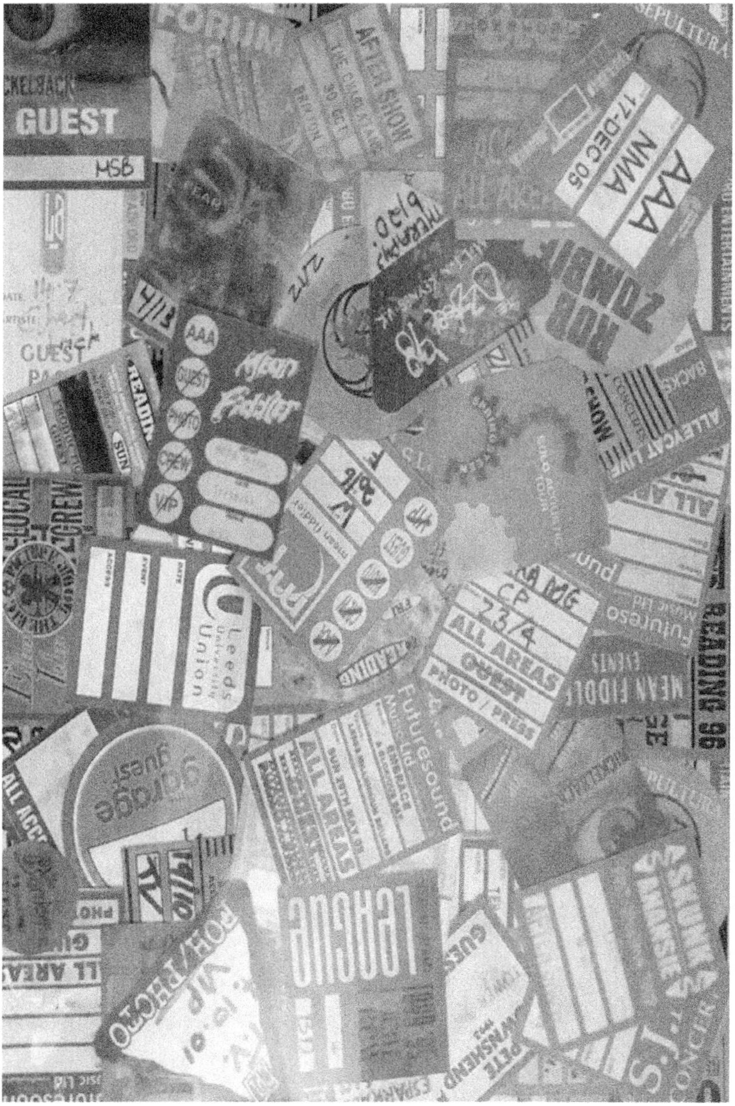
GUEST
AFTER SHOW
SEPULTURA
AAA
NMA
17-DEC 05
ALL AREAS
GUEST
PHOTO / PRESS
Leeds University Union
Futuresound Music Ltd
READING 96
MEAN FIDDLER
ALLEYCAT LIVE
LEAGUE
VIP

22

Preface

This book began life whilst being an in-patient at a mental health unit, so the style may dip into erraticism now and again, because quite frankly my mind is ~~weary and in the noisy push of confusion~~. There will be song references spattered throughout these pages like the blurred out Pixies one just then due to music being the only constant in my life, but because of publishing rights I can't afford the copyright to reprint them and so there's an added 'guess the lyric' game show element to this book.

Now would be the ideal time to reference the Bowie song 'Suffragette City' and the lines about being leant on and not having enough funds to pay the fine, but alas he wrote it and so I can't borrow it, even if it is just for added clarity. I'll give you cryptic clues as we go along as to what the song lyrics might be and armed with the discography at the end of this book; all you'll have to do is use your smart speaker or search engine to listen for yourself and work them out.

Think of it as an interactive publication where there's a soundtrack to read along to and you win the joy of music as a prize...who knows, you might just find your new favourite band!

I don't believe that I am clinically depressed, despite being diagnosed as having Dysthamia or Persistent Depressive Disorder (PDD), Adjustment Disorder and anxiety amongst other things. Maybe I'm in denial; but I've come to the conclusion that 'depression' is a word that gets abused and thrown around like confetti. Eeyore from Winnie The Pooh was depressed, Marvin from The Hitchhiker's Guide To The Galaxy was depressed - I on the other hand, just can't handle the real world.

Clue: *far out at sea you can observe the backstroke*

Hotel California

Aah...rolling hills, the sounds of sheep bleating and Grieg's 'Morning Mood' floating across the dales [cue record needle scratch]...well, there's none of that in The Valley.

I've always had this black cloud that follows me around and up until recently, my happy Sertraline medication had kept me more or less on an even keel. I was (still am) just too tired at the age of fifty to keep fighting with my own head day in/day out anymore and all it took was one world turning upside-down event to send me downhill fast enough, to try and take my own life.

Six days, one hundred hours of glucose, eighty hours of saline and some potassium later and the toxicity levels of my liver and blood got to a safe enough limit for me to be moved to a recovery unit. According to the doctors, I was still a suicide risk because I'd meticulously planned my own death – I'd written my Will, paid for the funeral and even produced an order of service...I've always been considerately organised like that. So, their recommendation was to give me a Section

Two under the nineteen eighty-three Mental Health Act and send me to The Valley.

My initial bewilderment that the health service had recovery units in the rolling hills of the Yorkshire countryside, where self-help groups and occupational therapy sessions would guide me on the road to wellness were swiftly dispelled, as I was deposited in what essentially appeared to be a low-level open prison. I was given a room complete with a rubber mattress, wardrobe shelving and a sort of en-suite bathroom, that I at least didn't have to worry about being shivved in.

Still weak and disorientated, I was duly swabbed and obbed and given the news that having successfully avoided Covid-19 for the past three years, I like pretty much everyone else, had contracted it whilst being on the main hospital ward and would have to isolate in my cell for the next three days. Like any seasoned traveller, I used the time to familiarise myself with my new surroundings; like checking for a Gideon's Bible, fishing down the sides of chairs for change and trying to make sense of the mini-safe combination mechanism.

Everything in the room had been thought out to minimise the chances of you becoming a repeat offender: the shower curtain rail was magnetic, so that any hanging weight upon it would cause the magnets to disengage and the plastic mirror; like all the fixtures and fittings; were torque screwed to prevent access to sharp stabby things.

The plugless basin taps were elongated to fill the bowl and prevent any comedic attempt at drowning and a single shower button dispensed water in fifteen second bursts, presumably to lower your chances of trying to water-board yourself. Alongside these protective measures, all personal items such as keys, belts, aerosol deodorants and charging cables were duly confiscated and a chit issued for the offending pointy, wirey or squirty contraband.

I quickly realised that being in here would probably make me worse before it made me better, based on the sounds emanating through the steel mesh covered windows and the adjoining corridors, but for now the Zopiclone, Quetiapine and Mirtazapine cocktail that I had been dosed with would send me off to sleep for a while. I awoke at around 3a.m. to a cry of "Help" filtering through the window; again..."Help" – same tone, same direction and so I got up and went to investigate.

There it was again in exactly the same format, almost metronomic in its frequency of eight second bursts (yeah, I timed it). Could it be a recording? Some cheap giggle from the night porter to keep us all cuckoo? For now though, fatigue took precedent and I closed the shutter and went back to bed with the words that the Eagles once famously sang swimming around my head – ~~you can check out anytime~~, "Help" ~~but you can never leave~~.

Clue: *something about being able to go, but inevitably being stuck there*

Screamager

I was awoken by an unscheduled room service call for more blood pressure, temperature and heart rate observations, which were abruptly postponed due to an alarm going off on the ward. I was to discover later that these interruptions would be a regular occurrence, due to some of my fellow inmates and their One Flew Over The Cuckoo's Nest attempts at freedom.

However, for now I had to be content with the continued cries for "Help" (he's five hours in now) and pacing circles around my room. As the day progressed, so did the alarms and murderous screams that echoed along the corridors – someone was obviously furious at something the voices in their own head had done.

I'd never had those kinds of voices, my internal dialogues were always whisperingly snide, self-deprecating or self-loathing to the point of humility and not aggression. Maybe I should scream; at least then I'd sort of be fighting back and not being beaten down by it until I was a sobbing mess. These screams though sounded adolescent, they didn't have the guttural depth that comes with age or experience, but more like a teen angst at being angry at the misunderstanding of everything the world is yet to show you.

I remember being angry as a youth, but not because of my own thoughts, but at the unfairness of society - the haves and the have nots, pollution, war, famine...things that couldn't be solved by listening to Sting harp on about cold war Russians or putting a CND sticker on your fish-tailed Parker coat.

I decided that in the absence of social interaction and the fact that ~~I had nothing to do but hang around and get wasted up~~, that I would construct identities for the faceless wonders that co-habited this establishment. I'd already decided that the young adult would be called Screamager after the song by the aptly named band Therapy? but I still needed a name for the guy who shouted "Help" every eight seconds - he's now done twelve hours without a break.

I decided that based on the nature of his one-word lyricism and that he was consistent in his time-keeping the ideal name for him had to be…Ringo. Being the stickler that I am, I worked out that he hit the third elongated "Help" at around the eight second mark and so there was no question that he was indeed a drummer.

It was only in the eighteenth hour of his repertoire that I decided that I hated the Beatles and likened them to some kind of Chinese water torture, as it tapped away at my head to the point of me violently and repeatedly hitting the mesh window in some vain attempt at repelling the letters H-E-L-P. Maybe I was wrong about Screamager and his pain threshold had just cracked somewhere around the ten-hour mark?

Clue: *being bored without a release*

Comfortably Numb

At this point, even as a placid individual...I'm losing my shit! It's only day three and I'm now cursing the eighty or so Paracetamol that I overdosed on, for not doing their job efficiently enough. How can Ringo the human metronome keep this going for so long? Was he conscripted in the Gulf war as an interrogative torture tool and now had PTSD? Was I being tested to determine my breaking point?

I was informed by the nurse doing my latest batch of blood tests that the unit was split into five sections: under 55's and over 55's male, the same for females and an additional unit for the dangerous patients.

Ringo it turned out; was directly below me in the over 55's ward and had dementia and the only word his brain had decided to stick on was of course "Help". I felt like a completely heartless wanker for loathing him – this poor guy didn't even realise he was stuck on a loop and was so frail, that they couldn't sedate him on ethical grounds or be sure that he'd wake up again even if they did. He should have been in respite care, but thanks to continuous health service cutbacks by money grabbing shareholders, the only bed available for him was in the funny farm.

I can't begin to imagine what it must be like for people whose loved ones are in a similar predicament; to slowly watch everything that makes them who they are ebb away on a daily basis until nothing is left but confusion or loss of recognition. Admittedly, it was humbling to realise that some people don't have a conscious choice about whether they want to live or die, but evidently not enough to help me begin to feel anything about myself –

I guess there's the argument regarding euthanasia about when a person no longer has a quality of life due to terminal illness or limited brain function, but in the case of Ringo; who decides? To those of us observing from the outside, it would appear that being stuck in an almost vegetative state would be unbearable but for all we know, without the aid of PET (positron emission tomography) scans, Ringo might be having a blast inside his own world. Does the vocalisation of "Help" correlate to what may or may not be firing off in his neuronic network?

Clue: *being pleasantly unable to feel*

If It Makes You Happy

I think that this has been the only time in my short-lived career as a long-time suicide risk (oh the contradictory nature of it all I hear you cry), that I'd try to take my own life because of despair. It's not a cyclical process or seasonal disorder, far from it. My last bout of clinical depression in two thousand and twelve; at which point even the psychiatrist at the time unprofessionally deemed me a hopeless case; wasn't down to despair or rejection but a combination of work stresses, nerve pain and new parent exhaustion.

I was a full-time teacher; about twenty years in and had recently become a father to the greatest thing that has ever happened in my life. I don't say this lightly, because I've experienced some pretty cool stuff like touring the world with rock stars to death roll car crashes. ~~[redacted]~~, but with the added relentless median nerve damage in my C5-6 vertebrae, I just couldn't take anymore.

I'd like to add that up until writing this, I haven't met a single person who has left the teaching profession in recent years due to the ridiculous pressures put on them that has once regretted it, or anyone who has raised a child and not thought that the sleepless nights were worth it...I just wanted it all to stop because there was seemingly no end to it at the time.

The only other instance that I count as a 'real' attempt at ending my life was in my twenties – it was a point in my life where I thought that I was finally happy and wanted to go out on a high, before everything as it inherently does, came crashing down again.

This section could easily have been sub-headed 'Hedonism' by Skunk Anansie – I was doing stupid crap, getting wasted, pissing everything up the wall and was oblivious to the fact that ~~just because it feels good, doesn't mean it is doing~~.

In retrospect, I probably wasn't happy at all and I'm sure there would be some Carl Jung perspective on becoming psychologically mature and my disharmonious mandala of the unconscious and conscious mind were somehow involved or maybe and more likely...I was just being a dick.

Clue 1: *wearing an item of clothing, performing for insects until needing a drink*

Clue 2: *deriving pleasure might still not deem it acceptable*

What I've Done

I was finally allowed to fraternise with the rest of the patients, albeit tentatively and of my own choosing at first, by only venturing out of my room for mealtimes and medication. There was a sort of routine to the day which consisted of breakfast at 8am, lunch at 12pm, dinner at 4pm, supper at 8pm; all of which were followed by queuing for medication on the respective hour later.

Admittedly, there was a bit of paranoia to my forays onto the ward – Did they know ━━━ ━━━━, that I'd tried to ━━━━━━━━ ━━━━━━ ━━━━ ━━━━? Where was I in the pecking order? Did I have to appear the most nuts, in a prison equivalent of picking a fight on arrival? Whatever the reasons, I wasn't ready to be talkative.

I limited myself to making cups of tea and scurrying back to the safety of my enclosure, not daring to linger in the TV room or participate in any of the occupational therapy groups. Mealtimes weren't much of a social issue, I didn't feel hungry and I hadn't been eating anyway, due to the empty soreness of my stomach. I've always seen food as functional rather than a gastronomic experience, which based on the offerings available on the 'school dinner' hot trolley was probably for the best.

I do appreciate good food and have dined in Michelin starred restaurants, but have never quite got past the belief that food is a source of nutrition and fuel. Maybe it's down to growing up poor and no matter how bland or tasteless the dish was, it was all you were getting and so you ate it. There is of course the grandeur of a filet mingnon, but for me it's on the same par as the simplistic charm of a white bread, margarine, fish finger and ketchup sandwich – I guess that you could always cut it diagonally for a touch of class.

So there I sat in my room, like some melancholy adolescent unable to focus on anything or be motivated to be somehow productive and interact with the outside world…at least I had the familiarity of Ringo and Screamager filtering through the afternoon air to fill the void. I did for all intents and purposes seem to have ~~all that there is to do~~ ~~erased~~, which for someone in my predicament is a curse rather than a godsend. Some would relish the downtime to relax, contemplate and maybe even pursue some calming pastime but as all good, lonely people know, having that much headspace only compounds the fear, insecurities and more often than not gives a platform to that naysayer of doom inside your head.

[put on ring-masters hat/cue circus music] Roll up, roll up and wonder at the majorly minor transgressions that have no rhyme or reason to contributing to the mess you have become...that time you couldn't face going to a social gathering, the person who never smiled back at you casually on the street, not having any change to buy a Big Issue – trivial on their own, but combined create a snowball of 'if only I'd just...' uselessness.

Clue 1: *rubbing out oneself*

Clue 2: *an abundance of free time*

The Day I Tried To Live

Having wrestled with a rabbit warren worth of insecurities, I forced myself to leave my haven and assimilate onto the ward with a foray into the lunch queue. Much akin to the midnight soup kitchens, the clientele was a mix of shambling corpses and the great unwashed, all with their unique versions of crazy.

I managed a few tentative nods of acknowledgement to a couple of the saner looking people in the line, before having to opt for one of the pre-heated delicacies served with a double potato product option and tinned vegetables that had been boiled to the point of being colourless.

I sat separately to everyone else, partly because of the odours emanating from some of the guests and partly because I didn't know if there was a hierarchy – I wasn't confident enough to be challenged as to who I was and what I was in for. I ate what I could palate before thanking the staff for the most I had eaten in days, despite acknowledging that it may make a return visit by the time I made it back to my room. The catering staff were in fact the ward staff, who were also the medication staff, the reception staff, security staff, cleaning staff and more often than not agency staff.

It was unsurprising then, that there were no 'talk based' therapy staff to deal with any mental health issues that arose, because they were already doing the work of five other people. It would transpire that The Valley wasn't really equipped to deal with mental health problems, other than to subdue you with medication and leave you to your own devices. A five-minute weekly ward round session with a doctor, where you were talked at, before agreeing to stay on pills seemed to be the only clinical intervention available.

So, I returned to my room with waves of nausea and sweat pulsating through me, after the shock of something just about edible entering my gut. I lay sobbing into my plastic pillow, still wondering whether there would ever be a point to being alive again and still hopelessly in love with the person who'd contributed to putting me here.

They weren't the sole cause of my deterioration and if I'm being honest, my downward spiral was always on the cards given my track record, but they were to some extent the nail in the proverbial coffin.

A million thoughts swam around my mind, which probably meant that the Quetiapine was wearing off, as I muttered to myself with no particular coherence about everything and anything with no hope of a resolution to any of it. It seems like the words you tell yourself,

~~anyone chooses to live up to that seems harder you~~

~~need~~ especially when you're a gibbering wreck.

Clue: *not meeting your own expectations*

Who Knew?

I'm not going to get into the why's and wherefores of why Karen ended our relationship as abruptly and as coldly as she did, because I'm not her and it would be unfair to do so. I can't begin to understand how living with someone whose mood goes up and down more frequently than a dime store hooker's underwear would be like.

I certainly wouldn't have lasted the fifteen years we were together if our roles had been reversed; having to continually pre-empt or second guess every action or conversation. I'm sure she had her reasons, but in my own head I was stuck in the romantic ideal that because she'd said forever, it meant ~~forever~~ ~~didn't it?~~

I guess that the erratic behaviours I displayed became too much of a consideration to spend the rest of her life with, even more so because I didn't know that I was doing it most of the time. Could she have handled it better? Probably. Could I have handled it better? Unlikely.

I've never understood why my own mother stuck with my dad right up until his death five years ago, so who knows why I expected my own relationship to be any different. My father and I were complete opposites in pretty much everything, so maybe I thought that by being everything he wasn't that it would somehow work out better for me. He wasn't necessarily a bad father, but he was most definitely a shit husband and role model – violent, abusive, unfaithful…all the things that I'd like to think I'm not.

As it turns out, when Karen looked up from reading the Guardian magazine that Sunday and systematically called off the wedding, broke up with me and asked me to move out, it wasn't because I was a shit other half it was just because of a…"It's not you, it's me" situation. I'm convinced now that it wasn't the triple whammy of events that broke me, but the loss of the ideal that I'd created in my own mind about having a family, a home and a stable future with the people I loved the most because that's all I'd ever wanted since I was as a kid.

Clue: *eternally but wondering*

Simple Man

I knew that I'd hit the bottom of emptiness and despair, when not even my son was enough to keep me here. It wasn't an easy thing to wrestle my conscience with; after all I was his dad and I was supposed to be there to nurture, protect and support him. Instead, I was a wreck and could only see that I was useless to him in this state and I'd failed him as a parent. A lot of these feelings came from my own insecurities of having an absent father when I was a kid – my dad was ever present, but only usually through prison glass for most of my formative years.

I grew up with more of an attachment to my grandmother, than with my own parents – they weren't bad parents, but our house wasn't what I perceived to be a home. My grans house was full of life, laughter and a real sense of belonging and I spent every moment that I could there from weekends to whole school holidays and often ran away across the fields when it was time to go back to reality. I think my love of music was engrained during those times and growing up in that large Catholic household, meant that there was a diverse range of vinyl records propped up against the 1960's Decca 898 Stereogram. Having a half dozen each of aunts and uncles also meant that there was everything from The Clash to Showaddywaddy and Johnny Cash to Thin Lizzy on the turntable with a bit of my dad's Nusrat Fateh Ali Khan thrown into the mix later on.

My dad was a middling gangster – not small change, but not quite syndicated and as a result I only really saw him in my adolescence during prison visits or under police guard in hospitals after some deal had gone awry involving blades or shooters. There's always a lot of emphasis put on positive male role models having an impact on boys, especially in education and sports, but I don't believe that to be true unless you're in an environment that subscribes to patriarchy and even then it would be a skewed perspective.

By definition, my own lack of having a consistent male icon should have resulted in me being a complete wanker, instead of just a mild one. A role model in my mind, is anyone who gives you positive guidance and pulls you up on when you're being a tool and that's what I got more of whilst at my grandmothers. So, when it got to the point where it felt like I wasn't going to be there for my own kid, all the deep-rooted cognitive psychological mechanisms that scholars write about in journals hit me hard.

It didn't help that my step-son Dean was angry at my suicide attempt either and he called me 'a selfish fucking prick' - understandable given the circumstances. The only explanation that I could muster was that it was easier to see a broken arm than it was a broken mind and I would still be his dad for as long as he wanted me to be.

I wasn't mad at him, I was mad at myself for letting him down and I had convinced my own mind that both Sam and Dean would be fine without me, because Karen was protective of them both. The one song that gave me a glimmer of remorse about leaving them behind, as if in some touching movie soliloquy was by Lynard Skynard and the lines –

Clue: *fret not, use your soul, be confident, my wish is for your contentment*

Battery

Going stir crazy in addition to the actual crazy inside my room, forced me to venture on to the ward again and to finally discover who the perpetrator responsible for all the alarms going off was. In the interests of anonymity like in the cases of Ringo and Screamager, I'll call this character Triple A for reasons that will become obvious.

Triple A was a self-harmer, but not in the conventional sense of hurting themselves by cutting, hitting or burning. It's true that they had employed these methods in the past, but had become more creative in terms of making preventative treatments less effective.

Intrigued and on the inquisitive side for potential methods to harm myself should the need arise again, I spent the afternoon with Triple A on the corridor of the ward discussing medication, previous attempts at ending it all and the colourful characters that passed up and down at intervals. Triple A wasn't in any way trying to end their life, they just needed to be able to feel something, anything - albeit more often than not, searing pain.

Triple A's arms, legs and face were a mixture of scars, tattoos, sores and piercings; all of which were indicators of the need to feel anything but numb. However, whether it was the lack of unused skin space or the buzz just wasn't doing it anymore, he'd adapted a more creative method.

The alarms were Triple A's escape attempts at getting to the nearby town to buy batteries, because the ward staff had gotten wise to him stealing the ones from the remote control in the communal TV room. As a follow-on result of Triple A's previous actions, anyone who wanted to change the channel had to request the remote control from the nurses' station and be supervised for its return, akin to a firearms officer signing out a lethal weapon.

Once, in his attempts to evade capture, Triple A had made it all the way to Leeds and was about to board a bus to his home in Thirsk, before being apprehended by the police and returned to the ward.

It's evident by now that Triple A got his name from the ▆▆▆▆ of choice for his method of self-harm and more precisely, batteries containing lithium. He'd experimented using various types of cell from CR button type, A23 and AA and finally settled on AAA in the absence of the lesser available AAAA – they just went down easier.

Apparently, alkaline batteries pose less of a threat to your health, as opposed to lithium ones which can cause renal, thyroid and nephrotoxicity symptoms – ironically, lithium is the main ingredient in treating bipolar disorders with the main side effects being nausea and diarrhoea.

However, the side effects of swallowing the batteries weren't the source of Triple A being able to feel; it was the removal. Each time Triple A ended up on the procedure table an endoscopy had to be performed, meaning that a camera had to be inserted down his oesophagus to locate the multiple batteries followed by a spring-loaded pincer.

Imagine if you will, a version of one of those grabber machines that you often find in seaside arcades, fishing around in your stomach and trying to scrape a battery back up

your throat for the prize. Everyone's a winner
– the doctor gets a tray full of free Duracell's
and the patient ends up feeling awful, which is
evidently better than not feeling at all.

Clue: *multiple power cells*

Save Myself

I've been assigned a Community Psychiatric Nurse (CPN) called Shelley, who is to be my guide and enabler on the journey back to becoming a functioning adult again. It's not a task that I envy, because at the moment I can't see a future to plan for, let alone the best course of action or intervention that fit my psychiatric profile.

Where do I begin when ~~I've been again~~ ~~between the devil and the deep~~ with no hope of making it back in sight? Everything is so clouded and jumbled that I can't focus on anything for more than a few seconds, or is it minutes? All the things we tend to take for granted like the daily routines of washing, eating, exercise, work, pleasure; all become lost in a pea-souper of brain fog.

Shelley explains that today's meeting is purely introductory and to get a baseline assessment of where I'm at. She asks questions like, "Why don't you want to be here?" and "What was the defining moment?" and I'm not sure of the answers, but she keeps pushing in manner that is strangely both unintrusive yet definite in its purpose. I try to tell her what I think she wants to hear, partly because I don't know the reasons myself, but that only results in her giving me a metaphorical kick up the arse.

I instantly like Shelley – at this stage I don't know whether it's just because she's listening, or that I get the feeling that she won't take any half-baked responses to her questions. I've always liked people more, who don't just take me at my word and push me to be more thoughtful or introspective. It's easy to brush off challenging questions with a witty quip here or a deflection there and so when people politely force you to think a little bit deeper about your response, then it's a signifier that they are genuinely interested.

I'm glad that I don't have to think too deeply though, because I honestly can't think straight enough to be contemplative and I'm pretty sure that she would see right through a falsified answer. Once Shelley has got an initial angle on me, she arranges another appointment to go through a stack of forms that will eventually become my care plan and set in motion the various agency cogs involved in this sort of thing. I am now well and truly someone else's responsibility, which is a good thing seeing as how I've demonstrated that I can't be responsible for myself – for the time being at least.

Clue: *stuck amidst evil and peril*

The Lost Art Of Keeping A Secret

Word had inevitably gotten out about my hospitalisation; partly because Regal Fail must have finally delivered my Will and associated documents to their respective recipients and the hospital calling Karen as my unchanged next of kin. I'm not criticising the frontline workers of the postal service; I was one of them until I had a fall during one of my rounds and was unceremoniously 'retired' because I couldn't complete my walking duties.

The job wasn't about the crappy pay and conditions – it was about the headspace and being outdoors, which for someone like me was the ideal remedy for keeping the grey clouds at bay, even in torrential downpours. Fun fact: posties wear shorts all year round, because it's easier for their legs to dry off and their calves are numb anyway from walking ten miles a day.

One such postal recipient was Jaspal 'Jim' Mundh, who I'd entrusted to be my officiant at my funeral service. I'd asked him to be an executor of my Will years ago when Sam was born and figured that he wouldn't mind the additional funeral duties, because he'd be involved in sorting out my wishes anyway. Jim was the first person to visit me in the hospital, before I was even admitted to The Valley, even though we'd probably not seen each other in about six years. As it transpired, he had phoned Karen when his copy of my funeral plans had landed on his doormat, rung around the hospitals and dropped everything to find me.

Jim and I are cut from a similar cloth and both have very strong opinions of what is expected of those nearest and dearest. I've known him most of my formative life, through good times and bad and he has always been ceaseless in his unflinching loyalty to those he holds true.

So, when he turned up at my bedside, the realisation of what I had done and the effect it might have on others hit me hard - how could I do this to someone who'd driven halfway across the country just to hold me? His fierce protection of me results in a barrage of questions fired at whoever will listen…"What are the next steps?", "How is he going to be supported?", "Which meds are you prescribing?" He's clearly shaken at nearly losing me and it takes whatever strength I have left to assure him, that the doctors are doing everything they can at this stage.

I'm so fortunate to have people like Jim still around – those friends that are more a part of your life than your immediate family, even though you might not see hide nor hair of them for ages because 'adulting' takes over and life gets busy. These are the kind of friends that pick up the threads of kinship as if they were only sewn yesterday, without any hesitation or reason to do so and this is what I put them through?!

I began to cry uncontrollably for no reason other than being overwhelmed with the realisation of how my actions could impact those that I would never intentionally wish to harm.

I don't know whether it's embarrassment, shame or regret but I plead with Jim, ⬛⬛⬛⬛⬛⬛⬛⬛⬛⬛⬛⬛⬛⬛⬛⬛⬛. He assures me that I have nothing to be ashamed about and how he's not surprised that it hadn't happened sooner, given that he'd pretty much been around for the majority of the crap I've faced in a relatively short amount of time. I don't claim to be anything special and there's not the smallest violin in the world that any index finger and thumb could play to make me think otherwise. I'm fully aware that in the greater scheme of things that go on in the world, my issues and those of the majority of people I know, are minute by comparison and if anything, I'm more fortunate than most.

The difficulty lies in how you're wired – for years the medical world has; through research and studies concluded that mental health issues were not just environmental, but the results of chemical imbalances in the brain. In altering these impulses through means of boosting serotonin levels and reducing network strand activity, a balance could be found to enable the patient to more or less function in a way that was conducive to managing a 'normal' daily routine.

It all seems like the test-tube mix from Huxley's Brave New World used to initially create a subdued Epsilon and then control them with soma and for the most part, chemistry-based intervention seemed to work.

However, more recently there has been a major shift in neuroscience thinking, in that although environmental, social and chemical imbalances are contributing factors, mental health issues are fundamentally hardwired into the brain. There is of course the matter of genetics and hereditary elements to consider similar to the ADHD trains of thought, but fundamentally the new belief is that it is essentially dicky circuitry that is in play.

So, the good news is that you won't have to rely solely on having your mind numbed; the bad news is…you're essentially fucked from the start and it's never going away. Still, the glimmer of hope here is now that you know this, you can get on with your life knowing that it's nothing you could have done differently to prevent it happening, but you can to some extent take control of how it defines you.

Clue: *please don't inform others*

Disciple

I've not heard Ringo for a while and have the fleeting worry that all my cursing of his cries for help to end, have through some divine intervention come true. Come to think of it Screamager hasn't been very vocal of late either, but I think that's due to him being dosed with the equivalent of a chemical cosh – an antipsychotic mix that is used to both subdue mania as well as to control seizures in dementia patients, so maybe they're both out for the count. The void in the noise department was quickly filled by a new patient in what can only be described as Harry fucking Secombe in an episode of Songs of Craze!

I loved Harry Secombe for his part in The Goon Show with Spike Milligan, Peter Sellers and Michael Bentine, along with his velvety Welsh tones on a Sunday afternoon backed by the Treorchy male voice choir, but Jesus Christ...this new inmate is relentless.

~~Don't get me wrong~~...I'm appreciative of a melodic choral voice, especially seeing as I'm both tone deaf and nasal when it comes to a good sing-a-long, but there's a time and a place. Unless you're in a bar, at a gig, partying or even at midnight mass, then belting out hymns not of the urban variety at 1a.m. is just not acceptable. There's a time and a place for How Great Thou Art or King of Kings, Lord Of Lords and every night at 1am is not it.

I'm pretty sure everyone in here is trying to get rid of their imaginary friends or at least stop listening to them, but this guy is regaling his in song. I don't have an issue with religion, to me it's the same as if you worship your morning coffee buzz or favourite item of clothing – whatever gets you through the day is fine by me…lord knows I've knelt at the porcelain altar of puke enough times. Although, right now with the absence of sleep meds, I am firmly of the belief that ~~god hates us all~~ to let this be going on night after night.

Clue 1: *don't misunderstand me*

Clue 2: *a higher power dislikes us*

Livin' On The Edge

I'm summoned to see the psychiatrist as part of their ward round. I think that I might have seen this doctor in two thousand and twelve, as part of my counselling sessions but I can't be sure. He seems pleasant enough and it's hard to take a dislike to someone who looks like the main character of an animated cartoon called Doctor Snuggles.

I get what will become the routine set of questions of whether I have any current thoughts of harming myself, before he delves deeper with, ~~redacted~~ Like with Shelley; I don't know the answer and I'm still too jumbled to have clear judgement and mutter something about being lost.

It's all a bit of a whirlwind and I'm being ushered out of the consulting room before I've had a chance to filter out the distractions of the tap of notetaking keys, hum of lights and clicking of Parker pens. It reminds me of the cycle courier 'Tyres' in the Jessica Stevenson and Simon Pegg sitcom 'Spaced' where every mundane noise translates as a rave beat...click, tap, click, tap, hum, click, tap, click, tap, hum and just like him, it's a beat only I can hear.

Apparently, I got lucky in having Dr Snuggles as my designated psychiatrist and by all accounts he is the 'good cop' to his counterpart, whom I am yet to meet but already have down as having the demeanour of Mr Blonde from Reservoir Dogs.

Clue: *can you explain your predicament*

Smoke 'Em

Despite Harry fucking Secombe arriving, there seems to be a core group of patients on the ward now, which creates a sort of stability in terms of familiar faces. Maybe we're full and the cohort of centres in the catchment area have a lack of demand, but whatever the reason it's provided a break to the anxiety of new socialisations.

Pretty much everyone in here smokes and like mealtimes, breaks are timetabled with the other wards so that the yard time prevents any mixing of potential trigger points. I don't smoke - I never really have, with maybe the exception of when I'm completely hammered - then you could put a twig in my mouth and I'd try and light it. However, I get that it's a habitual safety net or comfort blanket that accompanies both the melting pot of opinions and tobacco infused meditation and so I'd often hang out with the bad lads, inhaling second hand nicotine or cherry vape.

It's here that I get talking to Le Roi, who has been given the title due to being one of the longest serving patients on the ward. The king is pretty much institutionalised in terms of a cyclical existence of prison-social housing-ward-social housing-prison and our conversations often start like a recount by Uncle Albert from Only Fools and Horses, but rather than "When I was in the war..." it's more often than not, "When I was on C-Wing..."

Le Roi is one of those people that the system was meant to protect but ended up failing like so many others, in using punishment rather than prevention. A result of the excesses of free time and access to the prison library, meant that his encyclopaedic knowledge of both ancient and modern history was unrivalled but limited to outshining contestants on the late afternoon quiz shows on the common room television.

Le Roi was in this time on a thirty-day heroin withdrawal program and on shots of methadone as part of his nightly meds and the only vice able to calm his shakes in the interim, were the hourly smoke breaks... " was pretty much his mantra.

Judging by how some of the other patients reacted to nicotine withdrawal at missing their cancer stick slot by five minutes and thus proceeding to kick at the security door in the hope that it would somehow grant them a pardon, they could have used some of his wisdom.

The other drawback to missing your smoke break was that, similarly to the television remote, the cigarette lighter was on an authorisation only basis presumably to stop patients smoking in their rooms, rather than the more sinister motive of preventing a human torch episode.

This proved to be the cause of more frustration when an individual failed to return the Promethean article and thus creating an angry mob of unlit and unstable Richmond Blue aggressors on the hunt for fire. Fortunately, the ward staff were savvy enough to know who the likely culprit was and were able to retrieve the item before any 'death by a thousand Rizla cuts' occurred.

Clue: *use the items if you have them in your possession*

Jigsaw Puzzle

I've taken to doing jigsaw puzzles to relieve the monotony of being on the ward and to try and focus my attention span for more than thirty seconds and I've seen enough movies to know that it's the pastime of choice for people in institutions. There are a few games, puzzle books and pens in the dining room and when the door isn't locked; you can generally be in there between meal sittings for a brief respite from the busy corridors or the isolation of your room.

Given the limited range of the options available, I choose a gardening themed puzzle over one of an old British Empire world map and that of a panda chewing on eucalyptus – I don't do archaic patriotism or animals that identify as a bear and act like a cat...make of that what you will if you're of the jingoistic species assigning persuasion.

I didn't really want to use my Rolling Stones reference on a jigsaw, but there's a limited number of songs that directly relate to them. I would have much rather used my Jagger quota on Paint It Black, Mother's Little Helper or 19th

Nervous Breakdown, which would have been far more fitting for my situation as a whole but hey, ~~every single column goes without your consent~~ and ~~the best anything is the one time anyone genuinely bothers to notice anything~~.

Typically, I begin with edges and corners and build inwards – a strategy I'm assured is the most productive for speed and sorting based on Tammy McLeod's Guinness World Record of under ten minutes for a 250-piece jigsaw and not for the largest one of 551,232 pieces...this one's a standard 1000 piece.

Over the course of about three days, I sat and puzzled the shit out of that jigsaw; only to discover that right at the end that it had a piece missing – if that isn't a metaphor for my fucking life right now, then I don't know what is.

Needless to say, my foray into self-help was over before it had really begun all because of a tiny section of cardboard and to be honest, jigsaws aren't the most exciting of hobbies to keep your mind from distraction or to write about.

Clue 1: *you may not be able to fulfil your needs*

Clue 2: *attempting to complete a task before the weather changes*

The Man Who Sold The World

In the absence of talk-therapies on the ward, I seem to have become an unofficial patient counsellor to the rest of the residents. I don't know why people tend to gravitate toward me, maybe I'm not outwardly as bonkers as some of the others or I have a face that says 'tell me your woes, I've nothing better to do with my time' but for whatever reason I seem to have a steady flow of regulars with a couple of wild cards thrown in, that seem to want my guidance or advice.

One such character is affectionately termed the Latvian Loon and is somewhat of an enigma. LL without the Cool J preaches sixties peace, love, harmony and being at one with nature whilst sporadically punching glass windows, throwing chairs and attempting to hold the police at bay with a plastic fork.

He carries a notebook around with him that's full of inspirational quotes as a calming guide to keep his aggression in check, but the difficulty is that he never reads it and has usually thrown it at someone. I have no idea why he sought out my limited wisdom...maybe

I was the Natasha to his Bruce and telling him that the sun was going down, was like a suggestive hypnosis trigger – and yes; of course I tried it for a laugh.

We found literal mutual ground in the communal garden, more specifically with the maintaining of the planting beds and him needing something to focus his attentions on. I'm no Monty Don but I can generally pick out a plant from a weed and can cobble together a comparative analogy out of pretty much anything and relate it to a human characteristic.

LL's aggressive tendencies were borne of paranoia and that no one took him seriously and to some extent it was true; I certainly didn't and just thought that he was an attention seeking arsehole but more often than not, it's those types of people that do something horrific like plant bombs or go on a knife wielding rampage.

~~He said I was his friend, which seems an aside~~ because we would never have crossed paths without being on the same ward and you never really know which facet of someone's multiple personalities you're befriending. I guess it would be like being one of the kidnapped victims in a room with James McAvoy's character Kevin Wendell Crumb in 'Split' and not knowing which of the twenty-four identities you'd be getting.

I'd already witnessed 'The Cleaner' when LL first arrived – he'd frantically wipe and scrub all of the notice boards in the corridors and take posters off the walls. In the absence of any cleaning materials, he would remove items of his own clothing to use as dusters, which often resulted in him being a half-naked sweaty mess intent on de-sanitising the whole ward.

Another one of his less endearing personalities was 'The Collector' – this one would be obsessed with removing all the communal resources like books, felt tips and kitchen supplies (coffee and sugar sachets) and taking them to his room. He would then over the course of a number of days or until someone complained to the staff, proceed to sort, categorize and arrange the items into size, colour and expiry date order on his bedroom floor. Unfortunately, his attempts at being undisturbed and barricading himself in by using his bed were met with defeat, as the doors like the afore mentioned safety featured fixtures and fittings, were designed to open outwards and not in.

I've had my forays into obsessive compulsive disorders and it has taken me nearly thirty years to be able to leave a teaspoon in the washing up bowl until the next morning or not to sort my t-shirts into colour groupings and so I get where he's coming from to some extent. However, I will not be swayed on having all my vinyl records in not only alphabetical order, but also release date and separated into albums, twelve inch and seven inch singles – E.P.'s and ten inchers are still up for debate, but generally they go with the twelves.

So, whilst having my horticultural knowledge tested like some RHS version of University Challenge I manage to distract LL with the simple yet fragrant scent of a lemon balm that has taken over one of the raised beds. I've checked and they definitely have lemon balm in Lithuania, so I'm not sure why it's such a life changing revelation to LL who instantly goes to find his notebook to begin documenting this new discovery. He has a moment of frustration when he isn't able to enter the building without supervision, but to the Occupational Therapists credit, they manage to rope in a colleague to undertake the duty.

A while later like some exhumed Percy Thrower, I'm explaining that Melissa Officinalis has many uses and can be grown quite easily at which point LL stops furiously scribing in his notebook and begins worshipping the bushy perennial herb in the manner of a bowing acolyte. I'm all for Pagan worship of Mother Earth, but dude...seriously? I suggest that he might like to pot a cutting to keep in his room and spare the rest of us the possible next steps of him self-flagellating with a sprig of it and this seems to placate him.

Twenty minutes later and an entire page of step-by-step watering, positioning and supporting notes and LL bounds his merry way back to the ward, which brief interlude has hopefully given the staff enough time to relocate the communal items from his room back to their respective places. I on the other hand felt no sense of joy or achievement from my hour of recreational activities, but at least it made LL happy.

Clue: *claimed that I was a companion eliciting a revelation*

Only Happy When It Rains

Unlike the Garbage song, I don't revel in ~~feeling quite sheet feeling bad~~...I'd give anything just to feel something good for more than a fleeting moment – this however cannot be said for the affectionately named 'Toast' on account of the buttery delicacy seeming to be his only joy in life. Toast arrived on the ward from Rotherham, covered in wound dressings and stitches from where he'd taken a shard of glass to his arms, face and neck.

As Toast was later to divulge, according to the surgeon that patched him up, he had missed his internal jugular vein by mere millimetres thanks to those around him wrenching the object out of his hands in time. He would also reveal that feeling bad was the only feeling he was capable of...Toast blamed himself for the death of his daughters.

It's strange how the mind can shut down traumatic events for weeks, months and even years and this was the case with Toast. Both of Toast's teenage daughters had been killed in a car accident, of which Toast wasn't even involved in - he recalls at the time that he was probably at home watching TV or down the pub with his brother when he heard the tragic news. It was just an accident, an unfortunate event that happens more often than we'd like to acknowledge, only this one had happened to Toast ten years ago and the impact for him had only just triggered.

Maybe it could have been because he was staying strong for those around him, or he'd put his grief to one side and never really addressed it, but whatever the reason then had resulted in a catastrophic realisation now. The term PTSD and knowledge of post-traumatic stress disorder is still relatively new in terms of clinical perceptions, but nonetheless this is what Toast had been diagnosed with.

Like anyone who's suffered loss, Toast was no exception and blamed himself with a myriad of why's and wherefores..."If only I'd have given them a lift", "Why them and not me?" and feeling bad was his way of beginning to come to terms with his loss, rather than not feeling anything at all and trying to take his own life as a punishment for seeming uncaring or deeming himself a bad parent. The fixation with toast stemmed from having breakfast with his daughters on the morning of that fateful day and was seemingly the last time Toast had seen his children before their demise.

I remember sitting opposite him on many a breakfast morning on the ward and for the briefest of moments, his eyes would be filled with delight and as butter oozed down the corners of his mouth, he would be transported back to happier times.

* I know the song 'Toast' by Street Band would have been more apt, but lyrically the Garbage one makes more sense in context.

Clue: *deriving joy from sadness*

Orange Tree Roads

I've been encouraged to take part in Occupational Therapy sessions by the nurses, to which I reluctantly signed up for the Tai Chi with Chai Tea. I'm introduced to the therapists who all seemed to be called Sarah in some spelling derivative or other and I find a spot to begin my relaxation journey.

The peace is immediately shattered as the Latvian Loon bursts into the room bowing and scraping in a disruptive form of lateness apology, to join in the meditation and movement techniques. The next five minutes are spent with LL performing some over exaggerated breathing exercises and following his own routine, whilst the rest of us try and block him out by attempting to rotate an imaginary ball from left to right.

Sarah/Sara/Sazza are trying their best to keep the rest of the group on task with motivational descriptions like, "Imagine that you are

waving side to side…" but nothing can drown out LL, who has now developed his Tai Chi into throwing shapes like he's at a rave, leaving the rest of us wishing we were off our tits at an actual rave - anything's got to be better than putting up with his shit.

I've always been a bit sceptical about holistic therapies, but I think that it's because I grew up with the commercialised Western embodiment of them and I've always had an aversion to poncified ways of describing things - that airy, over superlative form of speaking rather than calling a spade a spade.

I strongly believe that a 'deconstructed beef patty on a lightly toasted bun' in reality translates as 'I couldn't be arsed putting your burger together and will charge you twice as much for the displeasure'. So, when it comes to someone is asking me in that manner to imagine that my negative thoughts are leaves floating away on a babbling brook, whilst holding an imaginary moon in my hands, then I'm going to take some convincing.

Through a sense of defeat or loss of chi, Sarah/Sara/Sazza decide to abandon the session and settle for brewing up the chai. I have some level of empathy with them from my teaching days, in realising when you're flogging a dead horse - there's always that one little fucker who thinks that they're the centre of everything and ours is LL. I've had chai before and so it's a nice hit of familiarity and because the ward is mainly full of scratters, it's rare that you can find a clean mug to make a cuppa even if you wanted to.

Clue: *stood in daylight in crops of wheat*

Bringin' On The Heartbreak

I don't think Karen's well and I mean that in the nicest possible way. I've racked my brains as to how she's broke up with me and some of the random messages that she's sent via text since I've been in here. I know that she was struggling with the early onset of the menopause, but the HRT patches must be doing something to alleviate her symptoms, instead of sending her batty? In fact, we used to joke about it being the other way around and me having the manopause, because I was the one who would have the radiator like hot flushes, night sweats and occasional forgetfulness.

Obviously, I'm no expert and can only base these observations on conversations I've had with Karen, articles, research and living with it. So, before the more militant feminists out there light their torches and sharpen their pitchforks, there is no offence intended about this life-changing time of womanhood that none of the male species could ever fully grasp.

The latest episode of her irrational states of mind, is that she wants me to remove all of my belongings from the house within the next two weeks, whilst I'm still an in-patient on the ward. I, being non compos mentis and unable to discharge myself due to the Section Two I was under, began to panic.

It seems silly reflecting back on it now that I was concerned; given that I was going to leave it all behind – I suppose that bequeathing your chattels is somehow more fulfilling, knowing that others would benefit from your possessions rather than thinking that your stuff is going to be bagged up and taken to the tip within the next fortnight.

It didn't make any sense; she knows where I am and why, but she seemed to be on a mission to remove any trace that we were once together from the house. This raised its own set of questions and further fuelled my paranoia that she had been having an affair with her boss – why else would she want shut of anything that belonged to me out of sight?

The further revelation that she had been to see a solicitor to try and remove my name from the mortgage, deeds and joint bank accounts and essentially take the house from under me for a nominal pay-off, also added weight to my suspicions.

Fortunately, in legal terms she couldn't do any of those without my consent because both our signatures were on the mortgage, but that wasn't going to stop her from unceremoniously evicting me from my own home in absentia. I tried begging, pleading, anything to try and get her to reconsider to the point where my friends Jim, Des and Sarah went round to the house to find out what was going on.

After what I gather was a mildly venomous exchange; Karen being told how unreasonable she was being and explained to that, she agreed to just the contents inside the house being removed for the time being. It wasn't an ideal, but it did alleviate some of the stress and anxiety she'd added to and with a set of friends like mine rallying round, it did provide me with at least some options.

It is important to note at this juncture, that there were friends from my old touring band days some twenty plus years ago, whom I'd only seen in passing at some anniversary gig or on the same bill of a festival or other, that stepped up with offers of storing the odd box here or there in their lock-ups, spare rooms or wherever they could find.

The likes of Rachael (lighting), Pete (sound), Jane (distribution) and Katie (merchandising) along with more regularly seen friends were all prepared to travel from across the country, like some riders of Rohan when Gondor called for aid. I guess that being from a time when music mattered and wasn't the disposable commodity that it is today, also came with the benefits of indispensable and enduring friendships that last as long as the miles you've put under your heels.

It transpired that it took longer than Karen had anticipated given her on-site work commitments, childcare issues and general everyday time pressures to throw my belongings in boxes – even if I hadn't been in hospital, she didn't want me in the house and opted to undertake the packing process herself.

As a result, I wasn't able to collect my possessions until two weeks after I had moved in to my new flat and so there was no need for any of the pressure placed upon me whilst still on the ward, needless to say when the time did come to move, my friends Geoff, Dee, Gordoooom, Des and Anna were on hand to carry the pitiful transit van load of boxes and bags into my virtually empty flat.

Clue: *apologetically, the fact is that you are causing distress*

Sweet Soul Sister

I've just received a tearful phone call from my sister Donna. As I've touched on before, we're not a close family and we generally don't see each other unless it's something like a funeral and even then it can be a bit hit and miss. I've been so used to my siblings only ever contacting me when they needed money or were in some kind of dire strait, that I had already decided whatever the reasons for this call the answer would be "No".

I had been burned time after time by my brother and sisters with loans of a hundred quid here or fifty quid there for a myriad of reasons at the time – "I can't pay my rent", "My washing machine has packed in" and so on, but ultimately the only real reason was...they needed the money for drugs.

I could be dismissive in that it was their own doing, or I could be found guilty of funding their habit, but the down to earth crux of the matter was that they had become junkies through my father. There was always heroin around the house in either dragon chased foil hanging from my nodded-out dad's fingers or neat little paper wraps stashed in books or drawers - any larger amount would be hidden under a loose floorboard by the fireplace. So, given that both my siblings still lived at home at the time and were around drugs on a daily basis, they inevitably gravitated towards them.

Donna had a shit life and it's no surprise that she got hooked on anything that could provide some kind of release. I honestly think that all she ever really wanted was to be loved and as a result, ended up getting pregnant to a bloke who said all the right things and then left as soon as he found out that she was up the duff. Her addiction pretty much began after her son was born and was initially sustained by my dad, until his habit became more expensive and as every good junkie knows, there's no such thing as sharing when you're that strung out.

I also believe that my dad used her addiction as a means of coercive control, so that she would stay at home as some kind of shameful punishment for being an unmarried mother. He never missed an opportunity to preach his half-baked Islamic ideals on the importance of family and so on, despite being one of the shittest practicing Muslims that I've ever met – that said; I've also met more than my fair share of judgemental Christians and the like. Maybe naming my kids with Hebrew monikers was some kind of subconscious fuck you to all of the pick and mix rules that he and so many others tended to adapt to their own agendas?

As I've explained, both Donna and my brother only ever got in touch when they wanted something and I knew that she was still using, despite the half a dozen attempts at getting clean she'd tried and I expected this to be another one of those calls to the cash cow. The conversation began innocently enough with the exchanging of pleasantries and the 'nothing much' daily routine questions before the tears began and I braced myself for the inevitable "Can you lend me some money?" request, that really translated as "Can you give me some money that I have no intention of ever repaying?"

"I've got cancer and they've only given me three months to live," was what she actually said. Stunned, I became silent to the point of Donna asking if I was still there...

Presumably from the years of inhaling toxins, smoking and having a generally unhealthy lifestyle her body was riddled with lung and stomach cancers to the point of being inoperable.

All of my predisposed judgements faded and all I could do was ask if there was anything that I could do. I couldn't tell her that I was sectioned or the reasons why and that I was in no position to accommodate whatever she was about to ask for, so I just listened and thought about the unfairness of me surviving and my little sister not. Yes, we had both made pretty shitty life choices – me attempting to kill myself quick and her choosing a longer more drawn out process, but not like this.

I'm okay with death, it's an inevitability – ~~~~ ~~~~ with health scares, accidents and near misses, but I can tell that Donna is terrified. I try to reassure her that people who have cancer often live longer than the doctors predict and if she made changes to her lifestyle that it would give her a better chance of adding a few more years, but deep down I knew none of that would work at this late stage in the day. In any case, her reason for calling, was to ask me to keep an eye out for her son when she was gone, to which I duly agreed – what else could I do? Donna didn't even last three weeks and that was the last time I ever spoke to her.

Clue: *time tricks those nearing death*

State Of Love & Trust

In fairness to Karen and in order to redress the balance of what you the reader might think of her, she has never once asked me for any form of maintenance payment for Sam. I had freely donated my Regal Fail severance pay to her to go towards the mortgage, utilities and general running costs to keep a roof over his head and to this day, she still hasn't used a penny of it.

I have of course being the dutiful parent that I am, additionally offered on many occasions to fund the shared responsibilities of school uniform, trips and general upkeep of offspring and all that comes with it and for the most part have been told "No" at every turn – although; that may change if this book ever gets published.

Maybe it's fierce independence, guilt or a sense of accepting responsibility that it was her decision to go it alone, but for whatever her reasons – I cannot fault her on her parental obligations. I have never once reneged on my devotion, responsibility or financial obligation towards anything family related and neither has Karen. We are both from the school of; 'if you do the crime, you do the time' – until your kids at least leave home and even then, the responsibility never really ends.

I do of course, ~~[redacted]~~ that keeps telling me that I'm not doing enough or that I'm a shit parent (I think it's called imposter syndrome nowadays) but then I'm reminded that being a parent isn't purely monetary. Yes, you need cash to provide a better level of Maslow's physiological and safety needs, but the most important aspects of the hierarchy are firmly rooted in the development aspects of your relationship with your child. It doesn't help me knowing all of this and my head continually questions whether or not he wants or even needs me.

I know the answer is of course yes he does, but that never stops the vine like tendrils of doubt from creeping into my thoughts. Hack at them as I might, I can never seem to get to the root to destroy them and end up instead, becoming an infuriated groundskeeper playing an eternal game of weed suppression.

I sometimes catch myself pacing up and down or expectantly gazing out of the window, hours before he's even due for his bi-weekly visits in a desperate attempt to speed up time in anticipation of his arrival. I'm sure that once he arrives, I must somewhat smother him in affection, much to the dismay of any pre-teen and I have to keep reminding myself that he's not there to be my emotional be all and end all.

There are inevitably the times when he doesn't want to come, because of a much more appealing gathering at a friend's house or monumental online gaming session with his peers and admittedly, it crushes me to the point of not being able to sleep.

I keep telling myself that I was the same when I was his age, much preferring the company of friends than hanging out with an adult and that it's just one of the stages a parent must accept in order for their child to grow and find their place in the world. I think that I finally understand the look of sadness in my own mother's face, when I had made the same choices in my youth, opting for a kick about in the park rather than an afternoon playing board games.

Clue: *being attentive to inner thoughts*

The Drugs Don't Work

I've finally been allocated a bed at a sort of halfway house, that's a stopgap between the ward and getting your own place. My CPN Shelley had been pushing for an allocation and I'd been on the waiting list for weeks, which further highlights the dire shortage of beds available in the health care system, but it does mean that someone else can get the spot they need at The Valley.

I'm lucky because from what I gather, most patients end up at a druggy hostel in Huddersfield and then end up being stuck there because statistically they're no longer a priority – not the greatest environment if you're already on your arse with a penchant for heroin. It's shit but the only option that most health care trusts are left with because of their duty of care; anywhere has got to be better than back on the streets, right?

The halfway house is part of a converted care home with rooms containing a single bed and bathroom and is the equivalent to the Four Seasons after being on the ward. I have never been as happy to have an actual bed with a real duvet, pillow and mattress as I am right now. The simple fact of having a warm safe place with the independence to make a space your own for a while has never been more appreciated and the best thing of all...it's quiet. No screams, no ward rounds, no slamming doors, no violence – just peace, with the only interruptions being your daily medication allocations.

I'm introduced to the staff and shown around the building; there's a communal lounge furnished with games, TV and stereo, a communal kitchen and dining room, a visitor's room and laundry facilities, all of which are accessible twenty-four hours a day with the only restrictions being no loud noises after 10p.m.

An evening meal is provided, but everything else is geared towards you redeveloping your independence and fending for yourself, presumably for the more vulnerable residents who have come from supported living environments – that said, there is a fridge full of snacks, sandwich fillings and so on with the only rule being that if it's got someone's name on, don't eat it.

The first thing I do is shower, an actual shower that's not dispersed in fifteen second bursts – I can't remember how long I was in it, but it was glorious. If I were a religious person, then it would be akin to coming up from the baptismal pool and being reborn – I think that I might have even cried a little bit over the sheer joy of normality.

I can't remember much more of that first evening, other than just sitting on the bed in silence for what seemed like hours and then sleeping properly for the first time in months. I must have overslept because I was awoken by a tap on the door at around ten o'clock by an apologetic care worker, to prescribe my morning dose of Quetiapine.

I think I recognise the worker from some heady days of youth and the old Bradford drinking circuit of punks, goths and rockers and so a memory lane conversation ensues and as it transpired, we did used to frequent the same places. Back in the day, Bradford was a veritable Mecca of music, particularly the genres that would be blanket termed 'alternative' and as a result had a massive sub-culture of thrashers, crusties and grebos. A lot of the big-name bands of that era and some that were to become global superstars, often opted to play in Bradford over Leeds, because they were always guaranteed a receptive crowd.

Bradford had already seen bands like the Beatles, Bowie and Queen to The Clash, Metallica and Muse all playing local venues and even spawned its own calibre of mainstream chart topping acts like Kiki Dee, Smokie, Southern Death Cult, New Model Army and Terrorvision as well as members of Girls Aloud and One Direction...most of which frequented the weirdo hangouts of the Frog & Toad, Wheatsheaf, Mannville Arms, Smithy and Fighting Cock. So, after listing pretty much every pub, gig, record shop and notable character from days gone by, her attentions turned to the more inquisitive nature of how I'd ended up in sheltered accommodation.

I'd already decided that I was going to be as open as I could about my mental illness, because quite frankly the historical method of 'shut up and get on with it' had spectacularly failed and so I began to spill the beans. Before I had even finished, I was met with "Ooh no love, never pills – it's such a slow and excruciatingly painful way to go." It wasn't the response that I was expecting at being asked how I'd tried to kill myself..." ~~————————~~ ~~——————~~ continued the support worker.

In the defence of the lovely lady, she was insistent that I only tell her what I wanted to and wasn't passing any kind of judgement and in all honesty I was glad that she had given me the most harsh and unsympathetic evaluation of my predicament that I'd heard. It was the kind of no frills 'dickhead' response that you would expect from a friend, after you'd done something outrageous or out of character and I was thankful for it, because it brought to light the cold, hard reality of what I'd done.

Clue: *a feline awaiting an imminent watery death*

Wandering Star

I suppose that after my 'dickhead' revelation from the care worker, now would be a good juncture to explain the why's and wherefores of my former suicidal plan. I am not promoting any form of idea or guidance to end your life in what I'm about to explain and would hope that if you've got this far into the book, that you would have already self-assessed as to whether you need to access mental health services or not. I guess the purpose of this is not only cathartic for myself, but to highlight that suicide is not an easy way out, as I had admittedly and wrongly thought so in previous years.

To get to that level of despair means that you have exhausted every possible avenue in your mental state that you could reasonably hope to find resolve and the only option deemed to give any kind of respite is to just stop being. The reason that I was/am such a concern to the psychiatrists is because everything was so rationalised, which defines you as a greater risk because it's not a spur of the moment decision that had been taken after an event; a contradiction indeed given that most cases of suicide are derived from irrationality.

I had decided early on that I would take an overdose, for no other reason than I was a bit soft and couldn't slice myself up or jump from a great height. However, that was not the only factor…my social conscience just wouldn't allow it, in that either of those methods would cause greater inconvenience and trauma to both my loved ones and the general public. No, a nice vomit and excrement job would be far less hassle than a road closure or blood-stained bathroom, which I'm pretty sure we can all agree would be in the best interests of everyone.

My Will was already in place from my previous episode a few years earlier and so a simple codicil update put that in order, but the funeral arrangements proved to be a bit of a nightmare. I had no idea that there were so many different ways that you could be disposed of and all the hidden extras and clauses for having a service like…'except on the third Tuesday under a full moon within a leap year' or 'any old ashes chucked in a box compared to a gold plated urn comprising of a laser engraved epitaph' – I guess the old adage that "funerals are for the living and not the dead" has some truth to it.

Once I knew that the legalities were in order, I began to research suitable places for me to depart. I knew that I didn't want to put my loved ones through finding my body and so doing it at home or somewhere near was out of the question. I'd seen corpses which were 'dressed' for a viewing at a chapel of rest, but none of them compared to the raw, brutal, first hand experiences of finding junkies that had OD'd when I'd been sleeping rough or seeing the effects that finding a body had done to a friend of mine, who had come home to find his girlfriend bled out in the bath-tub.

I'd thought about wading into the sea like a latter-day Reginald Perrin and swimming out until I was too exhausted to make it back to the shore, but then the thought of the seven years or so it takes for a missing person to be declared dead if I wasn't washed up onto the rocks put me off. It wouldn't have mattered to me if I became fish food, but I couldn't bear the thought of Sam not knowing for that long. So, blades, buildings and beaches were out of the equation and the only viable option left to me were pills and booze and so I began researching dosages, side-effects and locations.

It's at this point that I realised just how bad the privatised rail network is in the UK, which limited my options to get the last train both physically and metaphorically anywhere to my final place of rest. Honestly...it's really, really shit and just as bad on the buses – I'd sold my car a couple of years ago in an effort to be more eco-friendly, but that has now left me with either a massive hike or just calling the whole thing off. Given the current governments lack of regulatory intervention of all the things they've privatised and let go to pot, they'd probably spin it as a 'saving lives through shoddy service'.

I was left with two viable options; the Twelve Apostles on Ilkley Moor or Stoodley Pike in Todmorden, both of which were far enough away from the train stations and remote enough to only be accessible on foot by any emergency services - therefore maximising my chances of not being found in the dark until it was too late. I had thought of using the emergency function on my phone as a GPS locator and activating it as I felt myself drifting into unconsciousness, so that my body could be found before any ramblers, cyclists or dog walkers could stumble across my corpse and be traumatised for life – again, considerate as always. I anticipated taking a zip-loc food bag, in which I would place my phone, ID and donor card to make the whole recovery process as simple as possible, whilst I lay there ~~dying~~ ~~chuckling my knobby~~ and ~~holding a white for about my rescue~~.

Clue: *internally folded whilst being upset*

Check My Brain

It would be fair to say that given the introduction to this book, it would seem that I had carried out my plan, been discovered on the moors and taken to hospital, but alas that wasn't the case. Prior to my admission to The Valley and after Karen's triple whammy, I had sought the help of my old gigging mate Geoff to try and make some sense of it all.

Our families were pretty close and we'd often go on holiday together, meet up for drinks and have meals out and it just so happened that Sam had been for a sleep-over at theirs and needed picking up. So, I ended up sat in Geoff's garage - broken, sobbing uncontrollably and having seemingly lost everything in one fell swoop.

I couldn't understand it – there had been no arguments with Karen, no squabbles, no tiffs, nothing...we had been on a family holiday to Bulgaria the week before and had a great time – it was probably the most enjoyable, stress-free getaway with the kids that we'd ever been on.

Karen as I'd become accustomed to by now, was running hot and cold and seemed to be preoccupied with texting on her phone, which I later came to discover was her laying the groundwork for ending our relationship. It's irrelevant now as to who it was with; I had my own suspicions at the time, but it's all in the past and that's something that can't ever be changed and as my therapy sessions have determined - you can't be responsible for the actions of others.

After spending what seemed like hours sat on an empty flight case, that should have been housing a bass cab or something, Geoff had convinced me to check in with the Crisis Team at the hospital the following day. Karen had left me at Geoff's, refusing to allow me to travel back the twenty miles with her in the car for being 'pathetic', despite knowing how much I treasured our family unit and how she'd broken it, given the history of my own lack of home stability.

Of course, both Geoff and Dee offered to give me a lift, but I just needed to be alone and opted to be a double bus wanker for the next hour and forty-minute journey from Bingley to

Brighouse – besides, I was in no rush to return to where I was relegated to the spare room with immediate effect.

I hardly slept that night and got the bus to Sunnydale Royal Hospital the first thing in the morning on Geoff's advice, to where I had accessed the Crisis Teams' services before. I immediately broke down in the waiting room and was ushered into a cubicle where a series of questions were put to me – I can't really remember what was said, but because I had 'previous' and the unstable emotional state I was in, I was sat in a corridor until space became available.

~~~~~~~~~~~~~~~~~~~~~~~~ and I was so exhausted by a combination of fatigue and nervous drain that, when I eventually got a temporary bed somewhere in the yellow stage of the triage department, I must have fallen asleep.

I was woken intermittently by a steady stream of clinicians to assess my various levels of risk, ideations and psychiatric factors in and amongst the wails of pain, retching noises and other such A&E sounds emanating from the neighbouring cubicles. It was deemed that I was indeed a risk but would have to wait until a bed became available at a psychiatric unit, which could be anywhere from Halifax to Barnsley. Luckily, with demographics playing no small part, I was subsequently given my first admission to The Valley.

Clue: *weeping saturates skeletal form*

Chop Suey

Now...this is where it gets a little confusing, but hey; it's my messed-up brain after all! The parts that you have already read are somewhat of a sequel to this bit, because I had already been admitted to The Valley for a week on a voluntary patient basis. As a result of this, I was unable to make good on my initial plan to end my life, but instead began the steady decline further down my pit of despair, like Dante going through the twenty-four divisions of Hell without the guidance of Virgil or anyone else for that matter to walk me through it.

A psychiatric ward is not somewhere you go to get better and as any patient or nurse will tell you; being admitted just keeps you safe but it is not a place for you to get well...it's essentially a holding pen until you get to the front of the intervention queue. Normally, if you have been sectioned then you are not allowed the freedom to go outside unless supervised and even then, it is within the confines of the grounds. However, as a voluntary patient there are no legal grounds to stop you leaving and it was through this loophole that I was able to purloin the pills that I needed to kill myself.

Under the guise of going to the local shop which was a ten-minute walk away, I was able to gain the almost Willy Wonka like 'golden ticket' slip of paper that informed the check-in and security desks that you had permission to leave for a specified amount of time. The process involved a number of checklist questions about your intentions, how long you were going to be, where you intended to go and how safe you felt – all of which a carefully placed Stephen Fry-esque lie here or there would satisfy.

I knew that trying to smuggle alcohol in would be both immoral given the nature of some of the recovering alcoholics on the ward and also futile, because you were routinely searched for any such items upon your return. So, over the course of the following few days I would buy two boxes of paracetamol each day from the parade of shops; alternating visits to them so as not to arouse suspicion, whilst simultaneously covering up my patient wristband.

(Un)fortunately, there is a restriction on such medicines and retailers are only permitted to sell individuals a maximum of two boxes within the same purchase, hence why it took a few days to amass enough pills to be effective. Each box contained around sixteen tablets and I would hide a strip of each blister pack in the soles of my shoes, depositing the boxes and safety instructions in the nearest bin, knowing full well that I would be searched on my return to the ward.

The level of subterfuge that I employed meant that even with the most rigorous of checks on my return, there was no way that I as a voluntary patient would have raised suspicion despite my feet making a 'crinkling' sound when I walked.

On my return to my room, I then amassed the capsules into a small plastic bag and hid them in the paper towel dispenser in the bathroom, making sure that with some rearranging the window of paper towels looked full, to prevent the cleaners discovering my stash on a re-stock. I duly wrapped the empty blister packs in some of the afore mentioned paper towels and added them to the contents of the tearoom bin, which was emptied on a daily basis, to complete my deception.

I must stress that there is no way that the carers could have known what I was up to and I gave no indication that there was anything untoward...I lied, deceived and was secretive in a manner that a seasoned con-artist would be proud of. Such was the determination to end my life, that I could have charmed the devil himself without a hint of remorse.

The research that I had done prior to my admittance meant that to maximise my chances of organ failure, I would need to dose myself daily over the course of at least four days in order for the toxin levels to accumulate to a dangerous enough level...and so my demise began.

I systematically began to take the hundred or so tablets that I had stored over the course of the next few days, battling the waves of nausea that came with ingesting so many at a time as well as my prescribed medication and the bonus Zopiclone sleeping pills that masked a lot of the symptoms such as sweating, shaking and disorientation. The side effects of

Zopiclone can ironically make you feel depressed, but can also make you delusional or hallucinate and is only meant for short term use, but I figured that it would make my transition into slipping away a little bit easier.

I don't remember feeling anything as I took each pill, I'd adopted an almost robotic mindset to try and ensure that I wasn't coming back, with the exception of twice – once was due to the nausea almost making me vomit and the second when a moment of sadness came over me that this was actually the end of everything – if I had any sense of Catholic guilt, I might have turned to God and asked, "~~~~~~~~~~~~~~~~~~~~~~~~~~~~~~" or something to that effect.

I had already emptied my shelving, packed my possessions and left a note absolving the staff of any negligence and so I went to bed, making sure that I was flat on my back as an additional guarantee that if I did eventually vomit, that I would most likely choke.

Clue: *is there a reason to abandon me?*

Nearly Lost You

I have no idea what alerted the nursing staff to me being in the throes of death or whether it was a fluke that they just happened to be on their supervision rounds at the exact moment I began convulsing, either way I was discovered.

I can't really recollect the order of the blurred moments that passed, due to drifting in and out of consciousness – I was on the bed, the floor, over a toilet and seemingly nowhere all at once. A vague memory of being held up and walked around seems familiar, but in the same instance I could easily have been floating in space. I vaguely remember it as a flurry of blurred faces, lights, alarms and ~~~~~~~~~~~~~~ ~~~~~~.

The next time I regained consciousness, I was laid in the corridor of the ward - I must have collapsed again and the carers had given up on trying to walk me to the main hospital building. So, there I lay covered in bodily fluids, shivering and sweating…a failure once again. It would transpire that due to the early hours of my inconvenient rescue, there was only a skeleton crew of porters on duty in the main hospital building and so I had to wait for a chair to be brought for the ten-minute round trip it would take to get me to A&E...they obviously thought that I could survive the hour or so it took to arrive.

On arrival in triage I must have lost consciousness again because the next time I came round, I was on a trolley fitted with a cannula and hooked up to some fluid IV's, presumably saline or D5W. I was asked some questions that I can't recall the exact nature of, before I drifted off again and then was woken periodically for more blood tests.

Once I was stable, I was moved onto a side ward and proceeded to have regular visits from the doctors, nurses and psychiatric teams and so dear reader; we are pretty much back to where we came in at the beginning of this story with the six days, one hundred hours of glucose and so on.

I was accidentally given a kidney patients medication and discharge notes on my return to The Valley, just because we shared similarities. I really hope that Robert from

Rastrick didn't suffer too much or need his eye drops either, because they had been mistakenly put in my bedside locker for about three days – at least he wouldn't be able to see how dark his wee wee was and be worried...silver linings, eh?

Given the strain that the medical profession is under and the amount of temps there are covering shifts, it's hardly surprising that that a mistake was made and I'd like to acknowledge my advocate Lisa at this point, who followed up the data breach with the ICO.

Clue: *a far away call, asking me to return*

Heaven Knows I'm Miserable Now

Since I'd been in the hospital, I'd lost my original room which is understandable given the necessity of how many lost souls are in need and I had been allocated one next to a young lad of about nineteen. I was back in isolation and although Ringo was still at it with his cries of help, the newest annoyance came from the next-door occupant who was soon to be known as Johnny bloody Marr.

I don't mind The Smiths as a whole, but I've never been a big fan, especially not of that right-wing moaner Morrissey – I just always wished they'd cheer up a bit. Yes, I know...says the bloke who's so fed up with life that he tried to top himself; but I didn't write a song about it now did I?

The Occupational Therapist's had allowed Johnny bloody Marr the use of an acoustic guitar from the recreation room, as part of his wellness action plan and in fairness to him, the boy could play and sing - except that everything he did was nearly at the world record tempo of 600bpm.

For those of you that are musically minded you will know that this is termed 'presto' which the uninitiated can deduce, translates as extremely fast. So, after hearing 'There's A Light That Never Goes Out' which should be played at a half time of 68bpm or 136bpm depending on what key you're in, at 'hey presto' speeds it became really, really grating.

I suppose that if ~~I was happy in the hour of a drunken hour~~ in a bar at 2a.m, then it would have sounded magnificent, but I'm not and it's awful. Incidentally, the best Smiths song that I've ever heard is 'How Soon Is Now?' but covered by a band called Hundred Reasons – I know loads of bands have done it, even my mates in Paradise Lost, but the Aldershot version stands out...sorry PL lads.

Clue: *pleasantly inebriated for sixty minutes*

Streets Of Philadelphia

One of the first few people to come and see me when I was finally allowed visitors, since I'd spectacularly kyboshed my freedom privileges by getting sectioned was my drumming mate Gordon, or affectionately termed Gordoooom because of the genre of music he played. Like most of my friends Gordoooom was the type of person who was just a genuinely beautiful soul, who saw the good in everything and everyone.

He could instinctively see that ~~I was knackered~~ ~~and battered and emotionally at half mast~~ and so he just sat and waited until I was ready. I don't think that we even talked about my overdose; instead choosing to update me on what was going on in the local music scene and the myriad of albums he was involved in playing on. Like a remand centre visitor, he was allowed to bring items in like chocolate, plastic bottled soft drinks and the only special thing that I'd requested – salad. Yes, salad.

As stated previously in The Day I Tried To Live, the meals were intended more to fill you up and less about nutritional value and after my daily intakes of starch, carbohydrates and sugars all I really craved was something green and filled with vitamins. As we spoke, I munched on the ready to eat bag of mixed leaf greenery in an almost orgasmic state – I swear that I could feel my body rejoicing at the sudden influx of vitamin A and I had almost finished the bag before visiting time was over.

Likewise, my friend Sarah was equally generous in providing divine food stuffs, bringing in things like wholemeal sandwiches and fresh fruit. I don't want to give the impression that I'm some kind of health fanatic, when I would ordinarily be a white bread and the odd banana kind of guy, but the sheer lack of anything that wasn't processed or reheated made the more healthier options seem like a forbidden temptation that needed to be sated.

Sarah also brought an unopened jigsaw after hearing my tale of the missing piece – a lovely five-hundred-piece coral reef design that when completed, Des and I commandeered a picture frame in one of the visiting rooms to house it in. As far as I'm aware, the underwater seascape is still up there as a parting gift and is probably the only complete jigsaw puzzle in the whole of Sunnydale Royal Hospital.

Clue: *unable to comprehend due to injuries*

Mr. Jones

We got another screamer on the ward today and the easiest way to describe him is a cross between The Green Mile's John Coffey size wise and the Michael Winslow Police Academy character of Larvell Jones, with reference to his ability to mimic pretty much any sound he hears. Mr. Jones was another one of God's disciples who the good Lord had chosen to forsake, afflict and abandon and had been admitted solely on his autistic tendencies having irritated the general public and those who cared for him needing respite.

He'd only been there a day and the rest of us were already twitching with a combination of nerves and annoyance. Every morning at six o'clock, Mr Jones screamed like some Lion's Breath yoga exercise without the calm element, before commencing at least an hours' worth of Gregorian chanting at the top of his lungs as some form of penance.

I ended up sat next to him during an art therapy session and was amazed how he could switch his vocal cords like some Mynah bird on crack to duplicate the sound of a hedgestrimmer outside to that of the ward alarm when Triple A scarpered.

There was no showmanship about it and he wasn't trying to impress anyone, it was just how he blocked out the rest of the world and coped with whatever voice was whispering to his inner self and when he wasn't being a household appliance or some other mechanical device, he hummed. I don't mean hummed as in stank (unlike a vast majority of the patients); he emitted a low drone similar to that of when a form of kids have a supply teacher and find irritating ways to delay any learning without openly calling out or throwing things.

As you can imagine, finding topics of conversation for a break in the incessant humming became paramount and pretty much everything from favourite foods to the characters in Adventure Time were up for debate with the only downside being that most of Mr Jones' responses were resounding one word answers.

"Do you like this band?" – "No." "What do you think about the Lionesses performance in Euro

2022?" "Good." I'm not into football - I fair weatherly support Doncaster Rovers as a matter of hometown pride – but I cannot fail to be massively more impressed than 'good' by the England women's team...none of that rolling about on the floor, faking fouls and dubious sexual conduct that the men's game seems to be all about, with kicking a ball being somewhere down the bottom of the list. I will however, without any respect for the dead still refute Maradona's 'hand of God' episode – unforgivable!

It's at this point that I'm duly dismissed by Mr Jones in him stating that, ~~redacted~~ - I don't think he likes me very much given his religious sensibilities. When asking about his favourite book, I had explained that I thought the Bible had some good stories in it, but was nowhere near as captivating as George Orwell's Animal Farm (not to be confused with the zoophilia sexploitation of the unfortunate Bodil Joensen film) and in saying this had in some way given me the mark of Satan.

I like the Bible as much as I like the Torah, Bhagavad Gita, Guru Granth Sahib, Qur'an and Tipitaka, but there is undeniably greater literary skill from the likes of Huxley, Poe and H.G. Wells.

Given my mixed up Catholic/Muslim upbringing and spending a chunk of my time with an unofficially adoptive Jewish mum, I can say with some authority that the main conflicting religions are pretty much all the same. I know that even in just saying that, I'm probably going to incur the wrath of the Israeli Special Forces, Kataeb and Hamas, but if you read the sacred texts they all have similar key players like Abraham/Ibrahim/Avraham, Jesus/Isha/Yeshua, Mary/Mariam/Miriam, Moses/Musa/Moshe and so on and all worship one God.

I have never been to Israel and therefore can't speak with any authority on the current conflict, but the debates, discussions and conversations I have had with people from all faiths are fundamentally in agreement that religion is corrupted by those who seek financial and political gain...oh and it's all the fault of the British Empire – great, now I've added myself to the far right hit-lists too! The circles that I mix in are a beautiful melting pot of beliefs, traditions and compassion whether you have a faith or not. I have Muslim friends who attend Bar Mitzvah's, Protestants who live next door to Catholics, old school Hindus with new school Sikh's and we fundamentally all agree that the only prejudices we have are whether or not you are a twat.

My dad was an anti-Semitic prick and I recall him once saying that Hitler hadn't killed enough Jews, which caused a blazing argument between us and me raising the point that he wasn't exactly the most Aryan looking African and would probably have been next on der Fuhrer's list. I sometimes wonder whether my choice to shun all religion, once go out with an Israelite girl and give my child a Hebrew name was indeed an ethical stance?

Anyway, I handed in my damp effort at painting an Autumnal scene to Sarah/Sara/Sazza and went back to my holding pen to contemplate the existence of higher spiritual powers and whether forty-two really was the answer to life, the universe and everything.

After some research, it turns out that it might be...the Gutenberg Bible printed with moveable type had forty-two lines per page, Harry Potter discovers he's a wizard on page forty-two, Elvis died aged forty-two and in the book of Revelations it is said that the beast will reign for forty-two months – a sacred text, some magic, a king and a devil...coincidence; I think not!

Clue: *produce art using a range of colours*

Ode To My Family

I feel like I need to exorcise the demon that is the past of my paternal father. As I've touched on before, he was a bad man back in the day and didn't really do a stand up job at either parenting or matrimony. I understand now that the things he did were probably the only way he knew how to provide for his family and with all due respect, we never really wanted for anything despite their ill-gotten means.

That said, I would have gladly traded everything we had to have had a stable home – we weren't loaded or anything, because he took more drugs than he supplied and so he never amassed the mattress filled bank balance of a kingpin, but there was always enough to go around.

It's difficult trying to recollect any happy memories, because there were so many incidents of violence and abuse that anything good was pushed aside, at least until I had escaped from him. Escaped sounds like I was held against my will and to some extent I was, not in the physical sense but in the sense of emotional and mental control. It was only until his death a few years ago that 'the fear' left me in just knowing that he wasn't around - I was forty-five, but such was the power he had held over me, that it's only until then that I felt like he couldn't hurt me anymore.

It was around this time that some emotional floodgate must have opened and I came to realise that, as a child I had often been used as a tool in his exploits or as a cover story in some scheme or other. I do vaguely remember a road trip sometime in the late seventies, around the time when Ayatollah Khomeini had outlawed women wearing mini-skirts and crop tops and began his campaign of Western hostage taking - I was the unsuspecting drug mule for the return journey on one of my dad's heroin runs.

We had to pay someone to drive us through an Iranian check-point, whilst I was hidden under the seats with my British passport (my dad had a Pakistani one) like some 'Canadian Caper' en route to Faisalabad and I was promised that on the way back, that I could have as much Turkish ice-cream as I wanted as long as I kept quiet.

An earlier memory was of a village wedding in Nāliwāla which my dad had been called to as the groom...he'd neglected to tell his traditionally minded parents that he'd married a white woman, I was his kid and my mother was pregnant back in Blighty with my sister Donna. In some dowry land deal or other, I was hidden away until the deed had been done and my dad had committed bigamy which was okay, because Islamic law is different to British law and so polygamy was allowed.

Imagine my mother's surprise when my stepsister Tina turned up in England six years later and was slotted into family life, as my mother was then pregnant with my little brother – needless to say, my mum didn't have any more children with my dad after that, but given his track record who's to say that there aren't any other hidden offspring floating around.

I resented my mum for a very long time as an adolescent and some way into adulthood, because I could never understand why she stayed with my dad – again, religion reared its ugly head and her Catholic beliefs that she had made a 'for better or worse' pact with God meant that she just had to suffer it. I had witnessed my dad punch my mum through glass doors, drag her by the hair into the street and abuse her so many times, that when I was old enough to stand up for her, I got the same. It was no use going to the police, because domestic violence was normalised back then and even if we had, it wouldn't have made any difference.

Part of the reason was because there were so many corrupt officers in the police force at the time, that most of the CID were either supplying my dad's drugs from raiding his competition or were taking back-handers from him, which gave him an almost immunity from any wrongdoing.

That was of course until the price of back-handers inevitably went up, at which point we were subjected to weekly early hours raids, with officers even dragging us terrified 'Paki' kids (who somehow didn't count as minors or humans) out of bed on a school night, to antagonise my parents enough to add 'assaulting a police officer' to the charge sheet. So, as my dad started serving time, money got tight and the community gossip mill went in to overdrive.

I am still emotionally scarred from when I was in middle school and I was suddenly not allowed to go round to my mate Andy's house anymore, because I was the lad of that drug-dealer. It was nothing to do with Andy, he was nine just like me and not in control of such decisions, but the impact of "My mum says you can't come for tea anymore," was devastating.

It wasn't just incidents like my dad being in prison and my mum struggling to make ends meet that affected me, it was also my dad's side of the family and their ideologies based around what 'a good Muslim boy' should be. I would like it known that any form of religion from my childhood was enforced and not a considered choice, if I didn't attend mosque I would be beaten – however, because I was the kid with a 'gora' (white) mum, mosque is somewhere I would also be beaten.

My relatives from my dad's side were always dismissive of me like I was a latter day Mudblood, which was in stark contrast to the loving acceptance of my mum's side of the family who doted on my every move. You can argue cultural differences until the cows come home, the truth of the matter was that Pakistani element saw me and my siblings as lesser human beings and not because of what my dad had done, because they had all been benefitting from his spoils for years, but because we weren't 'properly' like them.

I think that in some way, this is where my distaste for religion comes from – not from the actual teachings, but from the small number of followers that are selective in their interpretations of the written word and its application onto others. I didn't fit the fundamentalist archaic mould, unlike today...I liked heavy metal, dressed differently, grew my hair, had friends who weren't the same as their friends and they hated me for it.

I stopped going to family gatherings when my dad was in prison, mainly because he couldn't enforce it but ultimately to avoid the incessant ridicule and mob mentality that I was subjected to. It was okay for my siblings, because they were too young to comprehend it, but I had to take every snide remark, every sly kick and all the injustice that came with it.

Despite efforts to please them in the hope that they would relent and my adolescent angsty pleas of, "████████████████████?" ultimately falling on deaf ears, I became more withdrawn and as a result my relationship with everyone around me became one of solitude and loneliness.

My dad who was supposed to be my protector had lost me my friends, left me out in the cold (both figuratively and literally) and tainted my relationship with my devoted mum. I had hoped that his stints in prison would have changed his outlook, but as every convict knows, you learn more on the inside than you do on the streets and if anything, he came back worse. It has since transpired that he was still running an operation from his cell, with the rent-a-cop prison wardens being directed by some of his then retired CID mates...who says crime doesn't pay?!

On his eventual fifth or sixth time of being released, the house was full of his coat-tail cronies and many bottles of Scotch were on the go to celebrate his return. In seeing that his first born who was in his eyes 'a fucking long haired poof' (his words not mine), I duly had the shit kicked out of me and thrown out of the house – I think I was fifteen. If I recall correctly, not one of his friends attempted to intervene, even when my mum ended up with a black eye and a broken rib for trying to stop him.

I literally had on the clothes that I was wearing and seeing as I'd lost most of my local friends due to being 'that lad', I managed to find a doorway for the night. As I sat there shivering and hungry, I vowed that I would never set foot in that house again and a life on the streets would be better than being subjected to his abuse. Even until the day he died, my dad insisted that he never did such a thing, despite a handful of people contesting otherwise.

The nineteen eighties were full of kids who skipped school and so there wasn't much flack for my lack of attendance and the truant officer most probably thought that I was on glue like Zammo from Grange Hill or off with some slags from Rita, Sue & Bob Too. I was sure that my mum would be worried, but I wasn't prepared to go home to find out in case he was there and still raging and instead managed to beg some change and call her when I suspected he would be sleeping his hangover off. I assured her that I would be okay and managed to arrange for her to meet me with a bag of clothes and some food – I hid at the meeting point until I knew that she was alone and despite her best efforts to try and drag me back, I was out on my own.

I fortunately was a familiar face on the teenage music scene and had met some good people, so my days of sleeping rough were few and far between with the odd night of being hidden in a shed like Mr Stink from the David Walliams book or behind a pile of boxes in the garage, which made the hardship of bus shelters and squats a little more bearable.

There were a couple of older friends; Izzy and Holly who had evening jobs at Pizza Hut who would steal food for me (and pretty much everyone else) and their friend Lisa would let us crash on the floor of her nurses' digs, by sneaking us in through the kitchen window to bypass the student safety officer on the door.

I also had a girlfriend - surprisingly for a long haired poof - mysteriously called Mel with a silent X (I never knew why), who despite not being able to let me stay with her at the age of fourteen for obvious reasons, had pestered an older friend of hers, Marley to convince his parents to let me live in their spare room. I am eternally grateful to Marley and his parents for essentially saving me from a life in doorways and was saddened to hear of his mum's passing a few years ago.

I had remained friends with him for years later, until I eventually got tired of him continually letting me down – it was his parent's interventions that had kept me safe, with his initial prompt apparently being because he fancied Mel. It's rumoured that Marley and I fell out over a girl years later, but even though he had slept with She-Ra (not her real name or the long lost twin sister of He-Man) the real reason was because he'd barefaced lied to me about it...always thinking with his knob.

My dad did mellow with age, even to the point of once telling my little brother that he was proud of him for getting off drugs, as he comedically lit up another bit of foil in front of him. I don't think it was because he'd had a change of heart; I think that he'd just realised the extent of his frailty and not having long left to live given the years of chemical abuse he'd put his body through.

The difficulty with being a criminal is that you get old and there is always someone coming up the ranks who is more savvy and more brutal than the last and ultimately your empire crumbles to nothing...if you live that long that is.

I didn't mourn my dad's passing, there was no outpouring of grief. I dutifully went to the bizarre lockdown funeral, but more to ensure that he was finally gone for my own sake, rather than to pay my respects. The people who had taken me in and treated me with love, compassion and acceptance were more precious to me than he had ever been and it is those people that I still hold dear and respect (except Marley, the big fat liar).

My relationship with my mum is a little less estranged these days and I make a point of getting in touch once a week, I forgave her a long time ago because I'd realised that she was just as much of a victim as I was and if anything, I made it out while she was left there to pick up the pieces.

Clue: *am I visible or even valued?*

Big Gay Heart

You know that Matt Lucas character Daffyd who's insistent that he's 'the only gay in the village' well it turns out that he's not. A patient arrived on the ward with all the flamboyant mannerisms of Sam Smith without the entourage, which is absolutely fine but what does he want, a fucking medal (the patient, not Sam Smith)?

So what, you're gay and fair enough if you've only just discovered this and want to express your joy at finally recognising who you are then fine, but I'm pretty sure everybody knows by now from your incessant proclamations.

It's not his sexual orientation that perturbs anybody, apart from the God botherers of course, but the fact that he attempts to drape himself around you at every opportunity. I'm a hugger and so I don't mind, but what I do mind is that he quite literally pisses himself whilst doing it. I don't know why he's in here apart from his own admissions about drug use and hearing voices, but have some self-care brother. I know that hygiene falls way off the list of priorities when your head's a mess, I know mine did for a while – forgetting to wash, to change my clothes and so on but you cannot the dismiss the undeniable stench of stale urine.

The poor guy obviously has issues because when he's not pissing himself, he's urinating in the corridors, on the bookshelf and pretty much everywhere else like a tom-cat marking its territory. I did manage a sentient conversation with him that was virtually urine free, after he had forcibly been washed down and it turns out that he was traumatised from being drugged, raped and left by the side of the road which is where the police found him and brought him here.

It doesn't explain the pissing or maybe it does, who'd want to have sex with someone that repulsive – I suppose if your evil enough to be a rapist, then nothing would bother you obtaining your self-gratification.

The staff have taken to propping his door open because the smell in his room is making it almost uninhabitable, but they can't allocate him another room (if there were any) because he's a repeat pee-pee offender and would put two rooms out of commission. I managed a few more conversations with him and tried to reassure him that, "~~~~" but I've never been forcibly drugged, raped and abandoned, so what do I know.

He was still there when I left, but the hugs had turned to rage and he was having to be sedated for becoming violent towards other patients and he'd joined LL in his destruction of windows and doors. I hope he finds some kind of peace, but how could you after being violated with that level of abuse?

Clue: *over a period of time the pain may alleviate*

Don't Believe A Word

I've been allowed to charge my phone by handing it in at the nurses' station (I'm still not allowed wires) and have decided to try and research whether there are any references to being a fruit-loop in my family history. I know that there were undiagnosed incidences of autism and bipolar disorder in my uncles on my mum's side, but other than that I don't ever recall hearing of a mad aunty Doreen who lived in the attic.

As with any family, there are stories that could be just as well hearsay as actual truths and if every word was to be taken as gospel then by some estranged uncles, aunties, nephew twice-removed, whose budgie once shat on my great great grandfather is to be acknowledged, then I'm supposedly related to Elton John – that might explain my cousin's penchant for tantrums and tiaras.

So armed with the wards 0.4Mb worth of download speed, which was like trying to wait for that Pam & Tommy video from 1995 to pixelate and wondering whether you were looking at a foo-foo or an elbow crease, I began my very own version of 'Who The Bloody Hell Do You Think You Are?". In the words of the mighty Phil Lynott, "~~————~~" or something to that effect - here goes...

I was the product of a night out in the Locarno nightclub in Wakefield between Steve – a textile worker from Rhodesia and Christine – the daughter of a farm girl from the outskirts of Doncaster, which began my whole mixed-up existence.

I was born the same month Alice Cooper released Billion Dollar Babies, The Stooges beat every one into submission with Raw Power and Springsteen's first single from Greetings From Asbury Park, N.J. was Blinded By The Light – all very fitting, as I entered the world kicking and screaming. The song that was number one in the U.K. on the actual day I emerged was Blockbuster by Sweet.

The Irish Element: Richard Patrick originated from near Cork in Munster, a Catholic (of course) whose favourite hymn was 'The Old Rugged Cross' by George Bennard. Like many of his peers, he lied about his age and joined the British army for the wages, much to his fellow Republicans disgust. He was part of the Queen's Bays (2nd Dragoon Guard) cavalry, because let's be honest; if you're from that part of Ireland and you can't ride a horse then you're not a proper culchie!

He was involved in the Western Campaign in France, before being evacuated through Brest back to England and then re-deployed to North Africa, where they were amalgamated into the Royal Armoured Corps and equipped with Crusader tanks. He made it back; pretty much in one piece with only a smattering of shrapnel in his legs from artillery shelling and married his sweetheart Florence, who according to his parish priest was just as bad as the Nazis because she was a Protestant and he refused to marry them, so he moved to England to be with her.

After the war and like many people in the area, he became a coal miner and worked in the dark and dirty conditions until someone inconsiderately blew a tunnel with workers still in it and crushed his legs which prematurely retired him. I'll always remember that despite the shrapnel, the injuries, chronic gout and religious bigotry he would always walk the six-mile round trip to church for Sunday mass.

The English Element: Florence May was from the village of Rossington and one of those English rose type women, with a big heart, a strong will and the biggest sense of family. I can't remember whether she served in the Navy WRNS or the Army ATS, but either way she crossed paths with 'Tom Irish' as he was nicknamed (clever use of Tommy and Irish there) and threw her Protestant upbringing to the wind and produced twelve offspring – so much for the failsafe Catholic rhythm method.

I was pretty much raised by Flo until the age of four, in an often packed household of a mainly transient six uncles and five aunties. My own parents were working all the hours they could at Whitehead's textile mill in Laisterdyke, Bradford and simultaneously fixing up their first home, until it was habitable enough for me to live there.

The Indian Element: my grandfather on my dad's side of the family was a beanpole of a man called Ali, but he was always just referred to as 'Babu'. He was originally from India but went to work in Africa on the Mombasa - Kisumu Railway from the coast of Kenya to Lake Victoria. Whilst there with his wife Asmat, they had two children; Naz and Shabir (Steve) – the latter of which was to become my father and although my birth certificate states that he was from Rhodesia (which became Zambia and Zimbabwe), he was actually born in Nairobi.

I guess nobody in the Home Office cared what they put on your naturalisation form back then, because 'they all looked the same' in the eyes of racist Britain at the time, even though migrants; whether they arrived from the former colonies or on the SS Empire Windrush collectively saved the nation's economy.

'Babu' returned home with his wife and kids post 1967 and found himself displaced and no longer Indian, but Pakistani due to partition. He used the money he'd made working on the railways to buy some farmland and lived out his days producing sugar cane along with another two sons.

During all of this research I never once came across any reference to mental illness, but I guess back then it wasn't recognised and most of the people who were unstable were either lobotomised because they didn't understand PTSD or were put in asylums without any help until they died. It was comforting to find out that music had always been there and that I was born in a pretty badass month for new releases.

So, none-the-wiser but more convinced than ever that I can only hold myself together with my friends on vinyl, I started to look at how I'd ended up going down certain paths, having certain jobs and seemingly only ever having destructive relationships.

Clue: *what I say may be false or not*

Wanted Dead Or Alive

With the genealogy research seemingly hitting a dead end, I looked at whether the choices that I'd made throughout life might shed some light on my mental state and whether the jobs I'd done attracted or turned you into a 'certain type'. I've done some cool stuff that I never dreamed would ever happen to a nerdy little mixed race kid from the seventies, but I wonder whether it was luck, determination or a subconscious choice that led me down certain avenues.

It's no secret that music is my saviour and so there would seem to be an inevitability that I'd be involved in it in some way, but despite my love of music I am in no way musical and my time as a drummer was more from the school of one, two, many, lots rhythms than the technical geniuses of Neil Peart or Stewart Copeland.

In fact; I only became a drummer because:
a) I couldn't be arsed learning guitar chords,
b) I'm tone deaf and can't sing and
c) the band we started didn't have a drummer and I was the least talented.

I have played guitar, bass and triangle but drums were the instrument that suited me because lacking in confidence as I do, I could hide at the back. The rabbit hole of thoughts that you go down when you start recollecting this stuff is in itself mind-boggling and I tried to remember what bands I'd been in and if they had caused an impact on my psyche or how they might have influenced my own self-worth. All I ever did was play music and go to gigs – I wasn't into sports, I had no interest in cars or computer games – just music in whatever form.

I carefully began trying to make links between events in my life, what I was doing musically at the time and how it had affected me. I was the bass player in a band called the Funky Enzymes (don't ask) and they fired me because the drummer thought I fancied his girlfriend – I did, but I wasn't going to do anything about it...this in turn affected my self-confidence and how others perceived me.

My next bass related firing was from a band called Chorus of Ruin with the guitarist this time, again thinking that I was after his squeeze – maybe it's a vibe I give off? I wasn't interested in her and she was more like a sister...Webbo did apologise years later, but by that point they'd already released the single 'Headstone' and recorded the album without giving me so much as a credit on the sleeve.

My stint as a guitarist was very short lived as I couldn't actually play the guitar and let's be honest, a band with a name like 'Zippy Noise' weren't really going anywhere – although the Arctic Monkeys seem to have done alright...I wonder if Noel Gallagher ever coughed up that twenty quid to Jo Whiley, because he said a band with a name like that would never make it?

After over two decade's worth of drumming in bands like Green, The Letters, Voodoo Soup and The Slackers with my only claim to fame being that I was once nearly the stand in tub-thumper for Oasis on the Big Breakfast, I resided myself to doing the next best thing and became a roadie. I started off doing the swag (merchandising) for bands at gigs, lighting, rigging and eventually backline.

I've done everything from being sat cramped on top of gear in the back of a van on the M1, to setting up stages for the likes of U2 and pretty much everything in between – I had literally ~~seen a million faces~~ and I'd helped to rock them all! I have been more successful as a drum tech. (glorified roadie) than I ever have in a band and being on the road is the only place other than at my grans house as a kid, that I've ever really felt a sense of belonging.

Clue: *witnessed a multitude of likenesses*

Wasted Years

I think I had deluded myself whilst being on the road that it was happiness, like finding security in commonality – in that it was only present because of circumstance. I guess it would be the same kind of kinship as being a hostage, where you are forced into making the most of the situation and the people around you, except that I never wanted being on tour to end.

I still have friends in bands and as crew, who despise being away from home and can't wait to be back in the familiar confines of their daily routine – I never did. Maybe it's because I never had the same warm, security that comes with stability as them and had spent so many years running away from the torment and abuse, that being in transit was all I really knew.

Don't get me wrong; all the perks like travel, meeting people and hanging with your heroes are great, but being on the road can be full of the same mundane boring shit that you'd find in any job – the endless waiting around in venues, doing the same routine every night, putting up with other peoples weird and wacky mannerisms. For me though, just having that connection to the music made it all worthwhile, even if I could recite on cue the "You're the best crowd so far" spiel verbatim every night. It can also be very detrimental to your health both physically and mentally and if you're someone like me with an already damaged psyche, then it can be disastrous – and it was.

There were times that killing the mental anguish with booze, often meant that I would only know where I was in the world in what currency the per diems (daily expenses) were dished out in (pre Euros obvs.) It was all I could do to keep the cold harsh reality at bay between soundchecks and barrelling through the night to the next venue and it eventually took its toll when I began coughing up blood.

I'm glad to say that today's road crew are a lot more career minded and such ridiculousness is reserved for days off, but back then we all worshipped at the church of Lemmy, Ozzy and the Toxic Twins. The parts that I can remember (mobile phones were still fairly rare back then and ones with cameras hadn't been invented) would probably make you wince at their stupidity, but maybe they're stories for a different kind of book...I am still a bit fuzzy on how I woke up in a Bayswater hotel with nothing on but a champagne cork and a transvestite's wig?!

Maybe it's the traveller in me, or maybe it was the constant distraction of always being on the move and not having the time to stop and be alone with your thoughts – being on a tour bus with another fourteen bodies doesn't allow for much room to be a recluse, but I've realised whilst analysing it all for this section, that when all the coke and champagne wore off, I was just as alone as I had ever been. It still seems that ▓▓.

The internal loneliness and the self-loathing was always there, but I'm betting that some of you reading this will be thinking, "What's this twat got to be down about, he's had a right old life!" Yes, I have and based on how fucking amazing some of the stuff I've done is, it could appear that I've had it better than most, but that's getting into philosophy of what happiness is measured by. I'm not trying to justify myself or prompt for pity, but most studies on the determiners of happiness say that although certain things can enable a better state of mind, it is more likely down to your own personality or outlook.

I guess that it just goes to show that mental illness isn't just an affliction that affects certain types – it's not that selective in its brutality and certainly doesn't care what you've done, where you've been or who or what you are.

Clue: *not knowing oneself or one's actions*

Some jobs I have done that may or may not have affected my mental state:

- ice-cream man - demoted to the warehouse after one day in the van for eating all the Cornetto's

- sugar cane cutter in Pakistan - deemed unsafe after flailing around with my machete like Leatherface in the Texas Chainsaw Massacre

- shop assistant – sacked for purposely damaging Sara Lee triple chocolate gateaux's so that I could eat them as 'unsellable' stock

- journalist – let go because I wouldn't toe the party line and/or for refusing the advances of that smarmy bloke in editorial

- music reviewer – did it for the free gigs and albums

- roadie – best/worst life ever

- teacher – it turns out eight year olds and rock starts aren't that different

- dad – amazing, knackering, beautiful, heart-breaking

- postie – 'retired' by Regal Fail because I'd hurt my leg and couldn't walk my round

- writer – TBC

Self-Esteem

So, having looked at family history and work related history and not finding any causal links to my mental health, the only thing left to look at was the littered battlefield that were my intimate relationships of the past. I've never been confident around people, especially with the opposite sex...oh how hetero of me in a world full of rainbows.

I am still angry at the LGBTQ+ community for stealing the rainbow from the mild mannered hippies, who were too non-confrontational and polite to explain that they had already adopted it as an icon of peace, love and happiness. Shame on you gay community for oppressing others in the same way you've been oppressed – two wrongs and all that. Call me out on it like I'm J.K. Rowling if you like, but that doesn't excuse the fact that you've barefaced nicked it from a bunch of pacifists.

I've always seemed to pick as my mum would put it "wrong uns" and I don't know to this day whether I'm just inept at seeing my suitors with anything but rose-tinted spectacles or whether I know that they're bad from the off and I just like the danger. I am also, as I've been told, oblivious to others advances and have probably missed out on the "right uns" because I had no idea that they were in the slightest bit interested – if you're still out there BJCJ...I never stopped being besotted! Instead; my longest term relationships have been with pole-dancers, flight attendants, nurses and serial heartbreakers.

I was still touring when I got together with Alabama Tuesday – named partly by the Lynard Skynard song she always danced to and the day of the week she had off work for us to meet up. I'd been away on the road for a long time on and off and had just got back from a stint in Australia (not a euphemism for jail) when we hooked up.

I should have known that a girl this likeable, funny and great in the sack was going to be trouble...and she was. It was whirlwind to say the least with her falling pregnant about a year in to us being together and me moving in not long after. I didn't have much to move in, because I was living in a van outside a friend's house...what's the point of having digs if you're never there?

Inevitably, the heartbreak followed with us losing the baby through ectopic pregnancy and whether it was the strain or more likely that she was a slapper, we split up. As part of the grieving process, the bereavement team have a book of remembrance in the chapel at Bradford Royal Infirmary, where you can name your loss and leave mementoes for whatever stage they were at when the tragedy occurred.

I used to go annually for a very long time but stopped when I had found out that she had been messing around whilst we were together and there was no certainty that the baby was even mine. Still, I've raised enough kids to absent parents, that it wouldn't have mattered in any case – he would have been twenty-one this year.

Before Alabama, there was Diana...a beautiful moon faced student from a little village near Kendal, who I was introduced to by the singer in the band I was in. I'd rejected the advances from probably the hottest Special Constable that I'd ever come across (figuratively not ejaculatory) which was probably for the best given my family history and opted for falling head over heels in love with Diana. We'd been together for that university semester, when she went home for the Christmas break, but on her return in the New Year she confessed that she'd shagged some rugby player called Mark round the back of a pub.

I duly kicked myself for blowing it (again, not a euphemism) with the copper and being the needy little dweeb I was, as I explained it away to myself…at least she 'fessed up right? Needless to say, it festered in my busy little mind and eventually became too much to move on from and we split up – from what I gather she's had a couple of kids and turned into a right bitch anyway.

Karen in one of her past lives, as well as being a film extra was also a cage-dancer at the Torture Gardens fetish club in Soho. We'd got together years later when she was working three jobs and trying to raise Dean, after her husband had run up huge amounts of debt in her name and then left. I helped out as best as I could in and amongst marking and planning, with childminding, doing house repairs and trying to make it as easy as I could for her – I'd seen how hard it had been on my mum to do it alone when my dad was in prison.

Eventually, we got together and then Sam came along and things seemed to be going great until her job took off. I was overjoyed for her to be finally becoming independent again after so many years of paying off debt that wasn't hers and was immeasurably proud of the hard work she'd put in to developing her career. It was then that I started to feel like I was just a convenience; like I was just there to make her path easier. She stopped telling me she loved me and started telling me that she didn't need me and eventually ended our relationship.

I can't fathom why she had even asked me to marry her, got me to book the wedding and made me announce it to all of our friends. I am very much the type of person who doesn't accept things until the proverbial ink is dry on the paper and I didn't want to let anybody know that we had planned to get married, until the giving of notice and so on. Why do that? Why humiliate me in that way, if you knew that you weren't going to go through with it? I'm glad Karen is a success; she's worked hard for it but I also hope that the person that I found out she was having an affair with, is just happy to be her loveless financial retirement fund.

So maybe that's the answer as to why I feel the way I do – shitty people and not lineage or profession. Maybe I'm like an abused puppy that no longer trusts anyone, but the overwhelming desire to be wanted keeps me falling into the same situations and therefore stuck in a cycle of eternal sadness. ~~Who knows, does anyone in this game really know anyone?~~

Fuck knows, I don't have any love for myself let alone anyone else at the moment, with the exception of my 'be all and end all' of Sam and there was a point when even he wasn't enough. I can never let him know how much my whole existence depends on him – imagine the crushing amount of pressure that would be to anyone, let alone a twelve-year-old. God forbid anything bad happens to him, because then I genuinely would have lost the gossamer thin thread that I'm currently hanging on to.

Clue: *suffrage equates to displays of loving*

Low Self Opinion

It's ward round time again, but joining Dr Snuggles this time is his evil counterpart Emperor Palpatine. None of the nice twinkling eyes or welcoming smile just an air of indifference and a look of 'you've only got yourself to blame for being in here'. If this Palpatine bad cop was a shoe, then I'd be the distasteful shit that he'd just trodden in and it was my fault that he wasn't looking where he was going.

I'm made to feel like I should have succeeded in my attempts to take my life and reduced his caseload, maybe I don't deserve compassion for diverting valuable resources from the health service. It's not like I'd got pissed and got my head stuck in a bin or something, it was a genuine life-threatening incident.

Apparently, Palpatine is in tune with everybody's mental state and he declares that, "   " as if it's like a phase I'm going through. I'm essentially told what I'm thinking for five minutes, before being dismissed under the instruction that the Sertraline I was previously on obviously doesn't work and so I'll be cold turkeying and put on different pills. According to the nurse that showed me out, I'm told that, "He's like that with everyone" as some form of apology before the next unfortunate is sent in to the firing squad. I later found out, that Palpatine is not very well thought of amongst the clinical staff, which made me stop thinking that it was just me and that he was in actual fact a bit of a self-righteous knob.

Following my interrogation, I get to see Shelley again who has brought a Housing Support Officer with her. Karen has claimed that she would feel unsafe if I returned home, even though she had relegated me to the spare room and fitted a lock to what would now be her bedroom door. I honestly don't know what was going through her mind at the time, but it was more fucking unhinged than I was and I was certified, besides…it's still my bloody house too!

The main issue that had to be taken into account was that Sam was a dependent living at home and given my current state of mind, the only option left for me in the absence of nearby family, was to be put on the waiting list for accommodation – Karen had essentially made me homeless.

Anne was an absolute angel in every sense, compared to the devil I'd been in a consultation with five minutes earlier. She took my details, explained the bizarre banding process to which homes are allocated and that unfortunately the likelihood of me getting anywhere within the next eighteen months was like rocking horse shit.

I was advised to start looking at private tenancies, because the sooner I could avoid being sent to one of the hostels the better. So, after a brief catch-up with Shelley I went back to my room to look at the extortionate rental properties, that were double the amount in rent that I would be able to claim as a now single, jobless, homeless person.

I get that it would be weird to still be in the same house as your ex, but given that I'd literally been laid off by Regal Fail the month before, Karen knew that she had me over a barrel and that I wouldn't be able to make the mortgage payments alone. I wasn't broke, I was just broken and I had still been paying my way up until that point, so she was in no way financially carrying me like some lazy, scrounging other half.

I certainly wasn't going to disrupt the stability of Sam's home life more than Karen already had and so being of the mind that I wasn't going to be alive much longer anyway, it kinda made sense in some twisted form of logic that I was the one to not be there...some people really do get to have their cake and eat it.

Clue: *awareness of mental emotions*

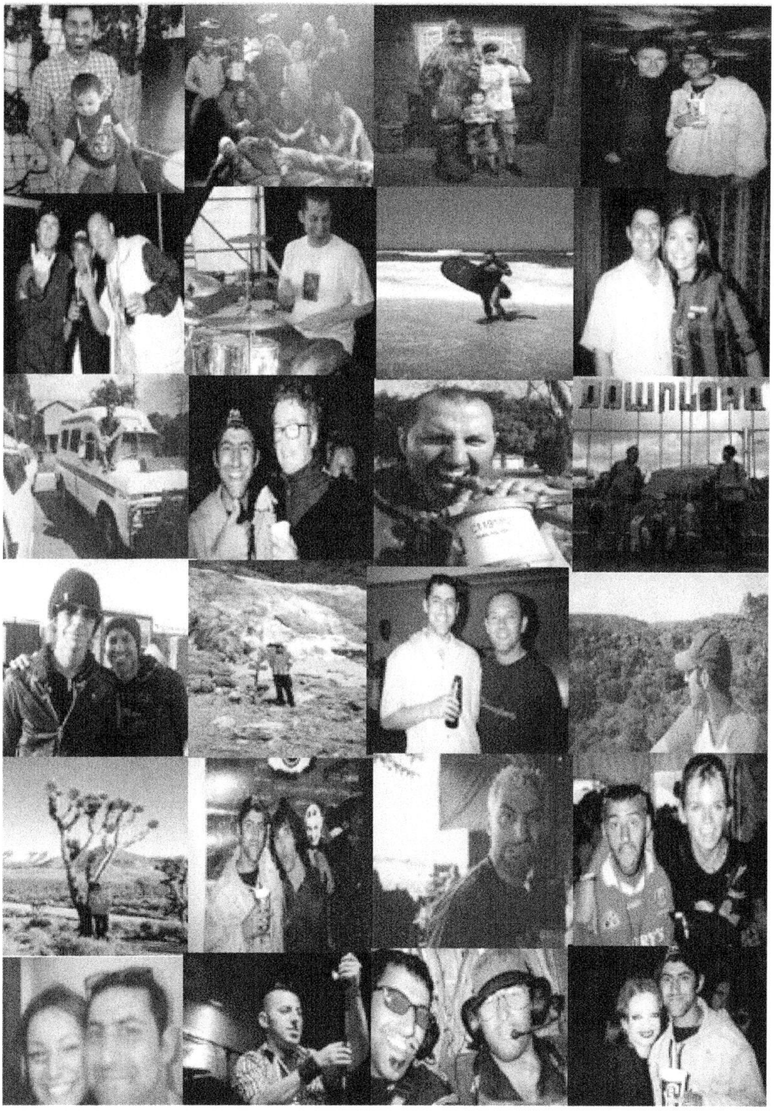

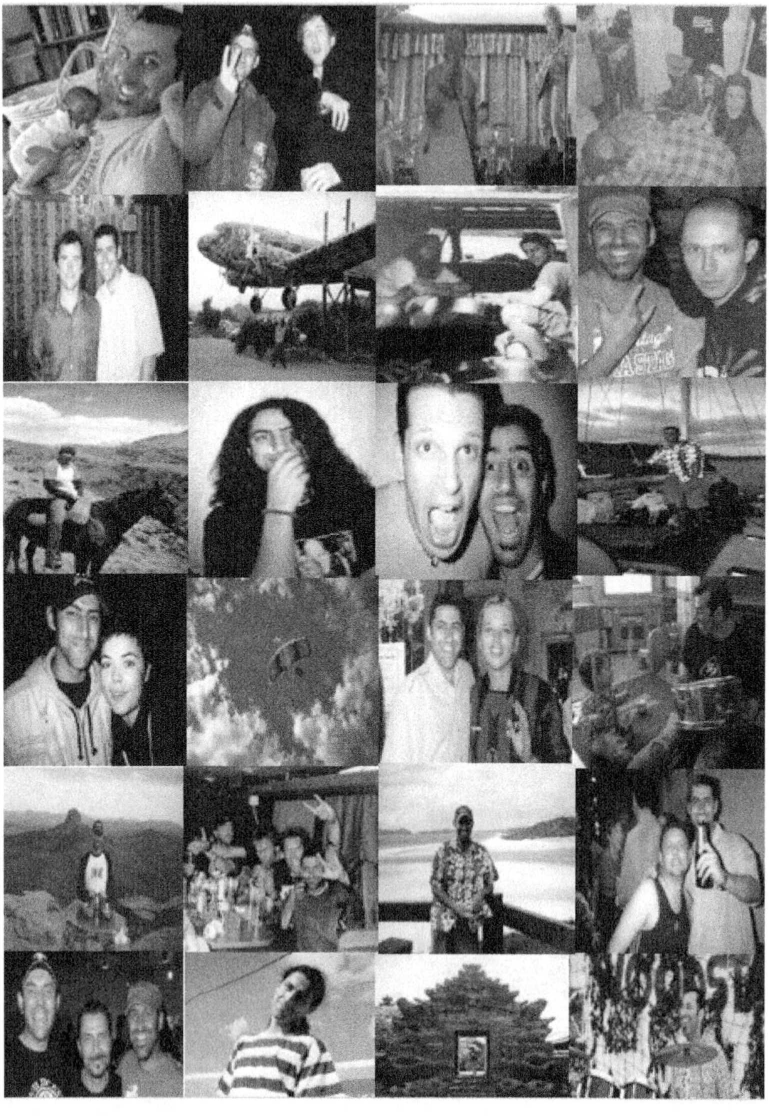

Bullet With Butterfly Wings

I have seemingly been taken on as an unofficial member of the nursing staff to provide counselling, mediate disputes and provide observations – now I know the health care system is fucked if they're letting the lunatics run the asylum. Maybe it's the ex-teacher in me, but the nursing staff have picked up on something that they see as a positive character trait, enough to put me in the middle of crisis situations.

Already seeing my stellar work with LL, who is currently responsible for all the door locks needing to be repaired because he's stuffed them full of coffee stirrers and snapped the ends off, I am asked to 'have a chat' with Shakey (not the actual one who sang about a Green Door, but just a bloke who shakes a lot from the DT's).

"――――," professes Shakey in the hope that I don't recognise the Smashing Pumpkins reference. It turns out that Shakey gets down about seeing himself as just a cog in the machine, at which point all the memories of shit six form poetry and philosophy groups come flooding to the forefront of my nodding and smiling demeanour. I'd seen enough self-help videos and documentaries to know that this is what you do for the cutaways and to feign interest in what is being said.

After hearing him witter on for twenty minutes about how misunderstood he is, whilst mulling over whether this counts as community service or a free counselling session, I offer the point that we are all cogs, but more in the sense that we all have our part to play…yeah, take that learned academics with your years of research.

A machine is only as good as the sum of its parts and if there's a broken or missing part, in Shakey's case a rat shaped cog, then it doesn't work or at best coughs and splutters its way through life. In negative terms, yes we are all cogs in a much bigger machine that we will never see the benefit of, as the grinding juggernaut of power and corruption only benefits those at the very top of the ladder – told you it was sixth form debate group material.

I have no idea where this next nugget of wisdom came from, because in my current state it doesn't hold any sway with me, but somehow it struck home with Shakey like some parting of the clouds and golden beam of heavenly light. "You're the most important cog in the machine even though you might not see the difference you make."

I know; vomit inducing right, but if it makes him feel better then who cares and it was just the shift in mind-set that he needed to start seeing his part in life as a worthwhile pursuit rather than a limitation...maybe I can become a life-coach when I eventually get out of here?

Clue: *I'm a prisoner regardless of my feelings*

Accidents Can Happen

It was a long-time friend of mine that helped me to realise that what I'd done didn't make me brave, selfish, loved or stupid but just human. Unbeknownst to me, they had planned to end their life by upstaging me in a more dramatic 'Thelma without Louise' manner.

Similarly, they'd made all their funeral arrangements, prepared letters to loved ones etc. with the intention of driving off the cliffs at Howth, north east of Dublin and letting the rocks and the sea do the rest. Luckily for all concerned, the healing power of music saved them with the lines '〰〰〰〰〰〰〰〰〰〰〰〰〰〰〰' that resonated enough for them to turn around and go home.

During my days on the Cloverdale ward, they'd flown over from Glasnevin to see me on what would have been my planned funeral day and I noticed the song lyrics tattooed on their arm – a permanent mantra for when times get tough again. I don't know what I'd have tattooed lyric wise, probably something Chris Cornell had penned, but then again he'd succeeded in topping himself.

Unfortunately, the same can't be said for another friend of mine who chose to drink himself to death. He'd been a drunk for as long as I can remember, but we all were for whatever reasons...it's just what you did right?

In hindsight we should have spotted the signs, but we were all too busy masking our own insecurities that we didn't notice until it was too late. Don't get me wrong; this guy wasn't a saint by any stretch of the imagination and if anything, he was a complete tool when it came to everything from parenting to fidelity.

I think he got away with it for so long because that's all anyone really knew of him – you know...that singer from that tribute band, brilliant live, they play all over the world, you must know him and if you didn't - then we all knew somebody like him.

I personally had fished him out of oncoming traffic years before, when he'd openly been shouting that he wanted to kill himself and even with that blatant declaration, it still didn't register that he might have needed help. Why? Because he was completely fucking hammered...again! It got to the stage where he'd damaged his liver to the point of no return, I don't know whether it was cirrhosis or just organ failure, but nonetheless we lamented his passing by, you guessed it, getting pissed – go figure?

Clue: *not your whole existence, just a part of it*

Psycho Killer

The police brought in a guy in handcuffs today who looked like he should be on Interpol's 'person of interest' list. I've seen crazy, but this guy's eyes were frighteningly like Charles Manson's and contained more multiple personalities than I could count – what's that saying about the eyes being the window to the soul?

The mood of the whole ward instantly changed from one of relatively subdued calm to a heightened sense of alert – crazy knows crazy and literally everyone in here had raised hackles as the air took on a deep sense of foreboding. The arrival of this one person had somehow tipped the balance of an already fragile eco-system and a tension akin to the way a prison riot breaks out filled every room and hallway.

It took the police a good forty minutes to be in a position where they could un-cuff the guy, so that he wasn't going to attack them or anyone else for that matter and they duly left him in the care of the ward staff. Unfortunately, because he had come in after all the consultants had left for the day, he wasn't able to be assessed and so the nurses were stuck with whatever information was in his file and unable to prescribe any further medication.

I was able to glean that this guy's medical notes meant that he should be in a more secure facility, but seeing as everywhere else was full he'd ended up here. Even the hardened stalwart patients of the mental health system were on high alert, as this guy refused to stay in his room and isolate, instead continuing the menacing campaign of terror that he'd been handcuffed for in the outside world.

I've been in dangerous situations before but no hold up, earthquake or melee had unnerved me to this extent – it was a whole new sensation. I think it was mainly down to the unpredictability of him as a person, like a lucky dip of who would come to the surface and for how long. Inevitably it kicked off.

Manson had gone in to the recreation room where the Occupational Therapy team were hosting a session of Xbox, board and card games, to which he duly went around disrupting by taking playing pieces and game disks and stuffing them into his pockets. Those of us who were a bit more confident than some of the nervous patients asked the therapists if they could retrieve the stolen articles, knowing that if some of the more aggressive inmates tried to get them back that it would probably end up in a brawl.

One patient who must have had some kind of violence based trauma told the therapist, "̶̶̶̶̶̶̶̶̶̶̶̶̶̶̶̶̶̶̶̶̶̶̶̶̶̶̶̶̶̶̶̶̶̶" but it fell on deaf ears, because the therapist was shitting it just as much as he was and instead called an end to the proceedings. I don't know whether it was the heightened sense of alertness or a predictive insight but all that I could think about was; he still had the items.

Normally, a Ludo piece, a draughts disc or a CD-ROM wouldn't be a big deal, but this guy was off the scale bonkers and I instantly though that they could be used for self-harm or to harm others...ding, ding, ding teacher brain. I duly informed the therapist on duty who was preoccupied with clearing the room and so after getting nowhere I went to find a nurse, like some prison grass spilling the beans for extra yard time or taking my newly found 'one of the team' role to an anally retentive level.

And then it happened. As the patients were leaving the recreation room Manson had snapped the stolen game disk in half and was now pressing the jagged point into another patient's throat whilst holding him in a headlock. The patient in question was one of the kindest, gentlest and unassuming patients on the ward and already of a nervous disposition.

Maybe this rabid animal had seen him as the weakest of the pack and picked him off like an injured gazelle, or maybe he was just the closest when the killer personality emerged. There's a reason why he was in handcuffs.

Alarms rang, staff mustered like a fire station roll call and Manson just stood there. I don't know whether he was listening to the voices in his head for advice on what to do next, or whether he had realised the futility of his situation. Either way he froze; eyes vibrating and flicking in sporadic movements, all the while holding the broken disk. Initially, we feared the worst as droplets of blood began to fall onto the floor of the corridor, but his hostage was still intact – Manson was gripping the shattered copy of the aptly named 'Red Dead Redemption' disk so tightly, that it was his own hand that was bleeding.

It became a stand-off like the end of Il Buono, Il Brutto, Il Cattivo: on one side a group of patients who were protective of their vulnerable brother, on the other an entire company of nursing staff and in the middle a scared rabbit in the jaws of a predator. It stayed like this for a while, as phone calls were made and options weighed – do we rush him and risk a throat slashing, do we disperse and leave him to finish his kill or do we continue to wait for the called in reinforcements? Suddenly and inexplicably, he dropped his weapon and fell to the floor.

Seeing his chance at freedom, his victim ran to the safety in numbers of his allies whilst the nursing staff subdued the perpetrator and locked him in a visiting room, to await the return of the police officers who had dropped him off in the first place. I don't know what happened to Manson after that, but he didn't return to the ward that he shouldn't have been on in the first place. The scared gazelle/rabbit/patient had to go through the ordeal of a victim statement, which more than likely added a diminished responsibility assault to Manson's charge. We returned to the once again relatively subdued calm of the ward, complete with celebratory urinal fountain from the only gay in the village – it doesn't rain, it pours.

I was enamoured with the solidarity of the other patients during the incident, who all put their own needs to one side in order to reassure another – maybe this is where I was supposed to fit in, this tribe full of morose misfits…I'd always been part of the sub-genre of freaks, geeks and outsiders after all. I do hope that Manson gets the help he needs, rather than being institutionalised like Michael Peterson in Rampton, Ashton or Broadmoor and ends up worse than before.

Clue: *my anxiety makes it difficult to be calm*

Stand Up

My old teaching assistant has come to visit me, not old as in age, old as in former…which speaks volumes about Karen's lack of compassion, who still hasn't phoned let alone visited since I ended up in here.

Lesley was the last teaching assistant that I had before leaving the profession full-time and I am sure that she won't mind me saying, that by the time we finally hung up our interactive whiteboard pens, we were both as jaded as fuck. It wasn't anything to do with the kids, but the increasing workload, internal politics and a head-teacher who was one of those 'in it for the status' and not for the good of the community types.

I loved working at the school and the majority of the staff who weren't drinking buddies with the Head, were some of the most right on people that I'd shared a stale Danish pastry with at one of the many mind-numbingly boring training days. The job was hard with actual teaching being way down the list of duties in favour of nutrition, clothing, counselling, crowd control and just getting the kids through the door. It's the same story across the land in state schools, with social issues spilling over into an already underfunded and under staffed resource. It just got to the point where I was spending more time worrying about other people's kids, than I did spending time with my own.

The kids were the only thing that made the job worthwhile and when we weren't feeding them, washing their clothes or finding a quiet corner for an over-emotional seven-year-old who hadn't slept; we taught. Lesley was instinctive when it came to the needs of the class and we would bounce cues of each other when someone wasn't quite getting it or looked like they were struggling – all it took was a subtly directed look or a pertinent enquiry for us to change tack or try it another way.

One of my best memories was teaching Maths to a kid who was a serial truant - I can't say anything; I was just as bad. This kid was the son of a local hoodlum and maybe that's why I had an affinity with him, but he had a deal with his dad who ran a spray and plate operation, where his dad would get the car and he could keep the stereo for breaking in - you can't charge a minor under ten years old with a crime.

If you're not familiar with the term 'spray and plate' it's pretty much how it sounds: respray a stolen car, change the licence places (usually stolen from another car) and sell it on. He was also prone to cut and shut scams, where two ends of different cars from accidents are welded together, which is a great way of recycling except for the lack of robustness.

Anyway, every day's a school day...on with the Maths. Now, for the more traditional amongst you this method of teaching a kid Maths may seem unethical or even unorthodox, but I assure you as any good teacher worth their salt will tell you, it's all about the context.

The deal this kid; let's call him Billy (not his real name) had going was that, as mentioned before he got to keep the ill-gotten car stereos. So, let's assume that the original price for the stereo new would be £80, but Billy can only get £20 for it off dodgy Dave – how much have you lost already Billy? Right, you take your £20 but you have to give half of it to your mate Jimmy (again not his real name) for being your lookout. You spend eight quid of your tenner on baccy and Rizlas, 'cause we all know that you smoke at the age of nine. How much have you got left? And for the doubters amongst you, the ethical part comes at the end with a "Was all that risk and hassle really worth it for two quid?"

I duly filled in all of the child protection forms, informed the police and Social Services, but I can happily inform you that Billy went on to pass all three of his Year 6 arithmetic and reasoning SAT's papers and the last I saw of him was on Crime Stoppers.

Lesley gave me the biggest, tightest and longest hug when she saw my dishevelled, pastey faced shell to the point where it hurt, but it was a good kind of hurt. I can't remember who cried more, me or her but it meant so much that she'd driven up from her new home in Skegness to see me. She had brought enough chocolate and sweets to put Cadbury's out of business and it was gratefully received, seeing as how I had not been allowed out to the shops under my Section Two restrictions.

We talked about everything and nothing and never one to pass up on trying to convert me to her favourite band Thunder, she proffered the line, "░░░░░░░░░░░░░░░░░░░░░░░░" and I understood the sentiment, even if I wasn't a fan.

Clue: *periodically you may blemish*

Don't Let Me Be Misunderstood

There's an ex-squaddie on the ward who has already been named G.I. Jesus for a combination of his build and his insistence on trying to convert everyone to the divine word of God after his apparent apparition. I get the impression that he's also a bit of a racist – can you just be a 'bit' of a racist? Is there a sliding scale of prejudice?

Anyway, I base these assumptions on him shouting fucking Paki's at the TV, when a news feature comes on about refugees trying to cross the English Channel. I've been called a fucking Paki and it's not nice, let alone wholly inaccurate for this particular group of desperate Syrians trying to escape persecution.

I immediately correct him, which only results in him telling me in an expectedly uninformed manner that they come over here taking our jobs, claiming benefits, while he works and pays tax in a full on Oswald Mosley rant. Given that there are some actual Pakistani's in the room, including a trainee nurse who seem intimidated by his stature and level of intensity and my belief that I have nothing left to lose at this stage, I cock both barrels.

I want it to be known before I start, that G.I. Jesus is the exception to every squaddie that I know, who are the most kind, helpful and usually the best pranksters of any of my friends. Right you racist prick...firstly they're not from Pakistan, they're from Syria – do I need to show you a map? Secondly, refugees aren't eligible to claim benefits unless they've been granted Asylum status and even then it only works out at around £5.50 a day to cover food, clothing, medicine etc. There is no such thing as a 'true Brit', we're an island nation who have been invaded more times than your mum's back doors.

No, that's unfair, I've never met his mum – I take it back. "Oh, so you're just going to let them all come over on their banana boats?" As an ex-squaddie, I would expect you to be able to distinguish between a carrier ship and a dinghy, unless you are of course referring to the recreational holiday activity of a thing that actually looks like a giant banana? It's at this point the trainee nurse went off to fetch a couple of the more burly looking agency staff incase it escalated.

I never have been able to know when to stop and shut up and so I proceed to quote scripture at him like I'm Jules from Pulp Fiction holding up his Bad Motherfucker wallet. I'm pretty sure in the Bible, in Luke or one of the other fellas it says something like, "Judge not and you will not be judged; condemn not and you will not be condemned; forgive and you will be forgiven" – I knew sitting next to Mr Jones would pay off at some point. G.I. Jesus is a little bit stunned and sits down, as if he'd forgotten what the whole debate was about to begin with.

I explained that heated debates were fine (partly to stop me getting my head kicked in) as long as we were able to accept each other's points and accept a different perspective. He explained that, "~~————————————————~~, but I've been off my meds." We had quite a nice chat after that, in which he disclosed that he doesn't actually pay any tax because all the work he does is cash in hand, he voted for

Brexit and the Chinese were to blame for the Covid outbreak. Still, at least he didn't kill me and he had a reason for not making any sense. It did leave me wondering why there seemed to be so many patients with religious fanaticism on the ward though.

Clue: *my erratic demeanour wasn't directed at you*

Adam's Song

I'm being allowed out on good behaviour, after serving my probation for not trying to top myself again. I am of course subject to the myriad of safety checks, which are somewhat more stringent than I originally remember them but for good reason...I had proven that I couldn't be trusted.

My chaperone Geoff had to come up to the ward for a briefing, before he was allowed to take me out for the three hours of freedom fun. I was nervous about being around crowds and so we opted for a fry up at a café in the grounds of Shibden Hall in Halifax, it was midweek and so it was guaranteed to be quieter.

Shibden Hall had been made famous by the BBC drama 'Gentleman Jack' based on the industrialist Anne Lister who lived there in the 1800's, but to us it was just a nice spot for a bit of breakfast and a walk. If you are a budding historian/feminist/nature lover then it is well worth a visit and there's loads of stuff to do if you have kids in tow, like a miniature railway, playground, boating lake and that's before you even get to the seventeenth century house and gardens.

I can't remember that last time I had a full English breakfast and it was heavenly – there's something about bacon that makes everything right with the world! After stuffing our faces, Geoff being the unassuming guy that he is, seemed a bit uneasy with addressing the elephant in the room that was my attempted suicide.

So, we did what we always did and talked about our shared love of music and bands – Geoff like Gordoooom, couldn't stop being in multiple bands and had played bass in the new wave of British heavy metal (NWOBHM) band Excalibur from Bradford. Since then, he's been in Slam, Voodoo Soup and is currently holding up the bottom end frequencies of the Fore Fighters (Foo Fighters tribute band), Alanish and more recently Rituals.

I get that it must be hard for Geoff nearly losing another friend, after the guy I talked about in the 'Accidents Can Happen' bit of this book was the singer in one of his bands. I break the deadlock by announcing that, "~~I never thought I'd die alone~~" which lifts the lid on the pressure that Geoff was feeling about wanting to know, but was afraid to ask. We decided to go for a walk around the park as a lunchtime rush bustled into the café, to spare the waiting customers the details of my foray into the afterlife whilst they ordered latte's and granary sandwiches.

I can't really remember what the order of conversation was, but I do know that we made each other cry – Geoff through unwarranted guilt that he couldn't stop his friend from slowly killing himself and me from the warranted guilt, that I'd nearly done the same thing again to Geoff. Before we knew it, my three hours were up and in the requirement to avoid a bloodhound search party through the woodlands of Shibden valley, Geoff duly deposited me back at the ward.

Clue: *I didn't imagine death in solitude*

Don't Shit Where You Eat

As if the corridors of piss weren't bad enough, there's now a patient that has to be put in adult nappies and not because he's incontinent. It wouldn't be so bad if once he'd filled his nappy that he changed it, but he just keeps it on and continues filling and filling until the faeces drops out onto the floor.

In addition to this, he also plays with it like he's in an episode of Dirty Sanchez, which is where his actual mental condition lies. If you're not well versed in the practice of a DS; basically any part of yours or someone else's anatomy is inserted into the anus, withdrawn containing poop and then a moustache is drawn using the offending residue on the face of whoever is nearest.

I don't know much about Scatolia, but it is linked to a whole world of difficulties such as obsessive-compulsive disorder, anxiety, schizophrenia, depression, bipolar disorder, ADD, autism or post-traumatic stress, especially if the trauma is related to physical or sexual abuse.

Needless to say, he's given a bit of a wide berth during mealtimes with the main reason being ~~redacted~~ and based on the way that he does eat. He's been given the unfortunate name of Gollum because of his resemblance to The Lord of the Rings character, or in his case The Lord of the Ring-piece (which is a different kind of movie).

It's difficult to describe Gollum's eating habits without sounding judgemental, because the guy has serious issues and it's not meant to be negative in any way about his condition, but it's hard to comprehend how someone has got this far into adulthood without any life skills.

Gollum can't use cutlery and so there is a radius off fallout from his meal the size of a nuclear blast, mainly because he misses his mouth more often than not and when he doesn't, he chews with it open. So, with a combination of the aroma and the second hand food, most of us have started to opt for the sandwich option and sit in the corridor, with the only difficulty being that there's only ever half a dozen pre-packed delicacies per sitting – you snooze you lose.

Another one of Gollum's charming attributes is that he picks fights and given that most of the people in here have an aggressive streak, it's not long before a scrap breaks out. After the incident with the hostage situation, we have been advised to just vacate the area that any incident is occurring in and so we watch from afar.

I don't advocate violence in any form and the guy clearly has psychological issues, but we are all collectively relieved when he is taken off the ward to a more secure area, even if it's just for the hallways to air out.

Clue: *refrain from defecating near food*

Fisherman's Blues

I've not seen Sam in weeks and my attempts at WhatsApp video calls, because the 0.4Mb Wi-Fi keeps dropping out have all failed. I don't think I realised just how much I missed him, until he wasn't around annoying the shit out of me at home. I'm desperate to see him and with it being his twelfth birthday this weekend, after some convincing Karen has finally relented to arranging a visit.

I don't want Sam to come to the ward – despite having visiting rooms, it is definitely no place for a child and even if it were, I still wanted to shield him from what I had gone through. Instead, I arranged another three hours of fun time leave and met them at a restaurant for a birthday meal - I've never once missed his birthday and I wasn't going to let being in the nuthouse stop me this year.

We opted for one of his favourite places and despite having the palate of a kid, he loves his food and chose the Mongolian restaurant that serves up stir fried kangaroo and crocodile. It was strange being here again; it had always been a family outing or celebration place to come and even though it was a celebration this time too, it all seemed a bit forced because Karen was there. She couldn't not be there, because we were still keeping up the pretence that everything was okay between us for his sake, but it was definitely strained on conversational topics that didn't include her destroying my whole world.

To minimise our interactions, I made more than my early-bird fair share of trips to the buffet and duly stocked up on greens and actual proteins, before I had to go back to the ward. I think that I might have over-egged the amount of hugs and cuddles that I gave Sam, but I knew that I had to get them in while I could, because without another reason for Karen to bring him for a visit, it was anybody's guess as to how long it would be before I saw him again.

It was gut-wrenching when it was time for me to go back to the ward, but at least I had a bit of ████ ███ ███ █████, with him ██ ███ █████ as I gave him the biggest squeeze that almost caused Skippy the bush kangaroo to reappear.

Clue: *brightness of mind, one held close*

Outside/Inside

I'd forgotten how much starting from scratch took out of you, especially when your head is a shed to begin with. I was released into the wild and had to start fending for myself, after so many months of being cared for – I ~~━━ ━ ━~~
~~━━━━━━ ━━ ━━ ━━━━━ ━ ━━ ━━━ ━━━━━━~~.

I wasn't ready to slot back into reality, but here I stood on the empty floorboards of my little one-bedroomed flat with only a folding camping chair and a holdall full of clothes to my name.

The flat itself apart from being bare was nice enough, compared to some of the holes that I could have ended up in. It comprised of a lounge/dining area, small kitchen, a decently sized bedroom and a small bathroom, but was still a far cry from the three bedroomed, gardens front and rear, Victorian semi-detached that I'd unceremoniously been ejected from. Still, it was what I had to try and rebuild my life from and in the absence of a bed (or bedding for that matter) I tried to sleep in the camping chair as best I could.

I was met the next day by Anne, who had managed to access some funding to get me some basic second hand furniture, including a bed, two-seater couch and a fridge – when I say that this place had nothing, it really did have nothing...the previous occupant had even taken the lightbulbs.

I was able to arrange some cheap carpeting for everywhere but the hallway, along with some curtains and a cooker and my new abode began to take shape. If it wasn't for the army of beautiful friends that I had arriving with a kettle, duvet and bits of crockery, then my second night in my digs would have been equally as depressing as the first.

It was strange waking up alone; I know that I had been alone on the ward despite pissy man's advances, but it was different because this is how it was going to be for a while. I had no intentions of jumping straight back into another relationship – how could I be with someone else, when I couldn't even be with myself?

The silence of not having other people sharing your space was strange and something that I'd never really felt up until now – Karen and I had been together for what seemed like forever. The silence in the hostel was more of a relief, than that of needing some level of interactive background hum, but this was a solitary kind of silence.

During the week Des, Anna and Ceri turned up every night after work to help clean, carpet lay and furniture move, so that I had a new beginning worth starting from and not some tobacco stained, blown floral wallpaper, floor-boarded shell that had been left by the previous occupant.

The finesse added to the painting and decorating was provided by DJi Digi (a.k.a. The Urbanizer) who specifically took time off from making his new album 'Forward' to help out. It reminded me of how the great comedians Paul Whitehouse and Charlie Higson began as painters and decorators, before their more prevalent talents as comedians were recognised.

DJi Digi is similar in that he's a multi-faceted musician, producer and actor, with the added bonus of having one of the steadiest 'cutting in' hands in the paint slinging business.

Clue: *not inside through no fault of their own*

Waking Up

My weekly routines now consist of: get up, ~~make a cup of tea, put the kettle on~~ and then either attending CPN reviews, online IAPT therapy sessions, still being on the waiting list for CBT (Cognitive Behavioural Therapy, not the bike test) and tentatively putting the feelers out for future work. I honestly don't think that I'm ready to jump back in to the world of a nine to five (~~what so ever to make a start~~), but I know that if I'm left with my own thoughts that it will only end in disaster.

Shelley is pro-active in keeping me occupied, knowing full well that if my overactive mind isn't stimulated, that I'll be back in The Valley before Easter and she has furnished me with contact details for everything from Andy's Man Club to the Countryside Alliance. I'm not too sure about sitting in a room full of blokes from my local area discussing how shit things are and decide that the only way that I'd attend, would be if it was somewhere out of town and more anonymous.

I've got a drummer friend Gaz who jointly facilitates a group and the work they do is great; it's not just for blokes either – the only other thing stopping me is the logo. I know it's the hand signal for O.K. but it reminds me too much of the 'made you look' game from Malcolm In The Middle and I don't think that giving a complete stranger a dead-arm on my first introduction would go down too well, especially if they got 'two for flinching'!

Due to the time of year, a lot of the outdoorsy stuff like allotments and woodland management are unavailable and so I register with a couple of charities as a volunteer. Given that most charities rely on a free workforce and can only run community based groups through funding, it's not surprising that everything in organisational terms is a little bit flaky and so weeks of emailing and phone calls back and forth, don't really elicit many worthwhile opportunities. It's okay though, because my sleep pattern is all over the place and I routinely nod off like a Nanna mid-afternoon anyway.

Sleep or more so the lack of it is a real problem, I can handle physical tiredness but mental fatigue throws up its own set of issues. Apart from the killer headaches as a result of not having any solid length of shut eye, I'm unable to communicate properly, lose my train of thought and my whole world ends up in slow-mo. I finally give in and try Sleep Restriction Therapy (SRT) which is essentially forcing yourself to get up at a fixed time regardless of how tired you are. The principle is that you stay awake and only go to bed at night when you are actually sleepy, with no snoozing, forty winks or other such napping allowed throughout the day.

The basis of the practice lies in the notion that all living things have a circadian rhythm, like flowers opening and closing with the daylight, nocturnal animals sleeping during the light and so on and studies have shown that if this rhythm is out of sync, then it can cause a whole host of problems. It's really common in nightshift workers whose superchiasmatic nucleus (SCN) in the hypothalamus is telling them that it's dark and they naturally should be asleep, but their body is doing otherwise.

There are some studies that show poor circadian rhythms influence the risk of psychiatric illnesses like depression and bipolar disorder, as well as the potential for neurodegenerative diseases like dementia, so with already having a broken brain, it's not the best news to discover.

I'll admit that the first two weeks were killer and I was going around like an extra in The Walking Dead; dropping things, bumping into stuff and generally not leaving the house after forgetting how to operate a simple door latch. The third week in though, things started to develop in to some kind of pattern – I made sure that I always got up at the same time every day, went to bed only when I was tired, instead of lying there staring at the ceiling for hours and stopped using 'blue light' sources by 9p.m. I don't know how much of it is biological and how much of it was habit formed, but it seemed to have some effect, in that I was sleeping through undisturbed.

It didn't always work though, because all it took was a little niggle to throw me off and send my mind spiralling to the point of being overloaded and then I'd be back to being unable to switch off and sleep. Tonight is one of those times and it's actually 3a.m. now, as I'm writing this. Part of the process is just to get up and do something productive, rather than try and force yourself back to sleep. The downside of it though, is that you end up going down YouTube rabbit holes when you're researching; although I have seen some great documentaries. I'm sure that the SRT is having some success, but I don't think that I can undo a lifetimes worth of insomnia in just a few short weeks and anything is worth a shot at this stage.

Clue 1: *prepare a beverage, play some vinyl*

Clue 2: *a means to earn a wage*

Last Christmas

For those of you who play 'Extreme Whamageddon'...it's okay, this doesn't count because it's only a reference and doesn't use the whole chorus. I don't play it; instead opting for my own twisted game of 'Which Celebrity Won't Make It To Christmas Day' and admittedly, I wasn't prepared for both Terry Hall of The Specials and Maxi Jazz of Faithless to be included this year, prompting repeat plays of 'Ghost Town' and 'Insomnia' much to the annoyance of my neighbours.

I'm not religious in any context, but then again not many people who celebrate Christmas are these days, if anything I'd be more in line with the Pagan celebrations of Saturnalia. I've never quite understood why people celebrate the birthday of someone they've never met, but any excuse for greed, gluttony and debauchery like a good old Apis worshipping sinner, right?

I still find it wryly amusing that Santa is an anagram of Satan, who in modern day terms actually promotes the denial of most of the Ten Commandments around this time of year – you just have to look at the crime, divorce, debt and keeping up with the Jones's statistics to see it in action, although murdering a turkey is debateable based on your dietary ethics and standpoint.

Despite my non-faith stance, you can't help but get swept up in the outpouring of reflection and hope that surrounds this time of year and given my still rollercoaster waves of emotions, I'm no exception. It was always going to be a bit weird to not be part of a 'traditional' family Christmas and seeing the kids open their presents on Christmas morning and after being together for such a long time ~~\[redacted]~~, like the wrapping paper on an unwanted gift.

Although Christmas Day fell on my shared custody weekend, I couldn't deny Sam wanting to be where his main presents, stockings and feast were and agreed that I'd have him from Boxing Day onwards, so that he could retain some sense of continuity.

I was never in any danger of being alone on Christmas Day, unlike so many other unfortunates who might treat themselves to a solitary mince pie or the special luxury of adding pickle to their cheese sandwich for Christmas dinner. No; I through friendship, good karma or just allying myself with wholesome people, was in no way going to spend the festive season sat watching repeats of Open All Hours or the novelty of a King's Speech (which hasn't happened since 1951) sat in my tiny one bedroomed flat, huddled in a duvet to keep warm and this was mainly down to one truly remarkably unremarkable person...Desmond Ernest Stow.

Clue: *she ripped to pieces*

King Of The Whole Wide World

I had known Des since I was at school and much like most of my other friends, no matter how many years or miles had passed by he was always there, ready to pick up from where we left off. Every time I had ended up on my arse from being beaten down by life's baseball bat, whether of my own doing or not, this guy was unflinchingly there to pick me up and dust me down.

I still don't know why he has remained my most loyal and dedicated friend to this day, because I don't think that I have done comparatively half as much for him, as he has for me...maybe that's the true test of friendship, in that it's not measured by deeds alone.

Des shares his birthday with Elvis (Presley not Costello) and so it's no wonder that his mantra also shared with the King is 'taking care of business'. His rock 'n' roll connections don't end there though - I vividly recall seeing a photo of him with Nick Heyward from Haircut One Hundred at his sister's wedding when she married their drummer Blair Cunningham, who coincidentally was born in Memphis about two hours' drive away from Tupelo where Elvis hip shook his way into the world. Blair had played as a session drummer with pretty much every notable band from Roxy Music to The Pretenders and Tina Turner to Lionel Richie back in the day and his daughter Ria (who I used to babysit) is now carrying on the showbiz mantle as a TV presenter.

So, it's unsurprising that this section is titled with an Elvis song from 'Kid Galahad' in honour of Des coming out fighting for me every time I need him because, ~~the man who can stay calm when his heart's gone on strike, will truly turn king of the whole wide world.~~

To say Des is unremarkable is meant in the most endearing way possible, in that he is what we often deem as a 'regular Joe' without whom the world would grind to a juddering halt. A shy, unconfident and humble person who rarely gets noticed and is always on the fringes of any social group, but they are the ones who end up being the most remarkable souls of the whole party.

I think that our friendship has endured partly because I've always taken and accepted him for how he is and that it's never been an issue socially or otherwise, due to our mutual respect for each other.

I would always invite him to gigs, aftershow parties and pretty much anything I was involved in, but would make a point of making him feel welcome, whilst others rubbed shoulders with the beautiful people and high society. He was my friend and not some hanger-on who was just there for the free booze and status and that meant more to me than some transient celebrity, whom for those I knew back then, have never checked in on me once during this whole debacle.

Maybe that's why we work; the fundamental principle of any lasting relationship is trust and we have always had that. It's not to say that we haven't had our bromance tiffs or quarrels – mainly over women, but not in the jealousy stakes. I think that we became so overprotective of each other, that no-one was ever going to be good enough as a respective partner with the annoying truth that Des was usually a better judge of people than I.

He would be guarded, considered and introspective about relationships, whereas I would leap doughy-eyed headfirst into destructive coupling after destructive coupling. If you don't believe me; he's been happily married for over a decade and I've only ever managed to get within months of tying the knot and settling down.

As soon as I was allowed chaperoned time out from the ward, with all the safeguarding checks about who I was with and where I was going for the three-hour intervals I was eventually granted, Des was there to provide a tentative foray back into the outside world. Whether it was just to sit on a park bench, have a cuppa or simply drive around because I was too apprehensive to be around people, he'd make an effort to see me at least once a week and call or message everyday (when I was allowed my charging cable back).

He'd even arranged a surprise visit from my friend Helen, who was over from Dublin and under the subterfuge of just meeting me for one of our weekly catch-ups and sprung her on me from behind a bush!

All the way through my incarcerations and subsequent rehousing, to where I am writing this now, there hasn't been anyone who has dedicated as much time and effort to ensuring that I stay alive. It is in no way a slur on any of my other friends, because let's be honest – once 'adulting' takes over then there are the considerations of work, kids, housekeeping and if you're lucky a little bit of time for yourself.

No; it is in no way an adolescent contest as to who is the 'bestest' friend or who has the most social media likes for their endeavours, just a cold hard fact that Des is one of life's good ones. I should really add a codicil to my will and leave him more than just my workshop full of power tools.

Clue: *a male who vocalises despite having nought, is the ruler of the globe*

Lucille

In one of Sam's weekend visits, he broke down and cried and it's the most heart-breaking thing that I've ever had to bear. Apparently, Karen who supposedly wasn't sowing the seeds of an affair while we were together, has had her boss Len calling round to the house 'out of hours'.

It's not uncommon to be friends with your boss, but when the distance to 'just pop in' from Norfolk to West Yorkshire is about one hundred and fifty miles or a three-hour round trip – you're not just in the neighbourhood...I guess he was just 'popping in' in another sense. I had to hold back all of my own hurt and pain, using every ounce of whatever strength that I had left, to not break down myself in front of Sam and be a parent.

I honestly don't know what Karen's deal is and to be honest, we're not together so it's none of my business, but when it's affecting your child to the point of them having to bear the weight of the burden put upon them, then it's not anything other than personal. What transpired over the next hour or so was all the hurt of parents separating, unwarranted guilt and the need for this pre-teen kid just needing to know that it was okay. It transpired throughout Sam's outpouring of mixed emotions that Karen was more or less leaving him to his own devices, buying him off with promises of gifts and generally just doing her own thing. I admit that my initial reaction was one of anger and even after weighing up that Sam was young and only as objective as his hormonal brain could be, that this still wasn't right – he's only twelve!

We talked, I hugged, kissed and comforted him all the while having to suppress my own pain that all of my suspicions that Karen had turned against me were true. The holiday in Bulgaria, when the kids had asked why she was always texting on her phone instead of joining in and she told them it was her boss about work – yeah, about working on my fiancée you twat. How, when she went on one of her cycling weekends, that out of all the cycle trails in England, she chose the Pedders Way in Norfolk.

The time I was left at Geoff's house to make my own way back, after she had aggressively demeaned me for even suggesting that she was having an affair. I don't believe that cheating on your partner is purely physical and after hearing all the things that Sam needed to get of his chest, I had lost any respect or remnants of love for Karen for all of the lies and deception she had committed.

Despite hearing how we'd 'get on like a house on fire', I have never met Len and I don't particularly want to, even though the likelihood is that we'll have to at some point. The old adage of 'it takes two to tango' is true and even though Karen was complicit in ending our relationship; he was fully aware that she was with somebody. Maybe they deserve each other as home-wreckers…he has a wife and two kids and Karen the mirror, well up until a while ago anyway.

Sam told me that Len was moving to Huddersfield, a mere and more convenient fifteen-minute drive away, presumably to make his divorce settlement a bit cheaper in not just shacking straight up with his mistress. It also wouldn't do to have the conflict of interest affect the 'family' ethos of the American I.T. company they both work for, so that they could stay in the same team and continue to have extra on-site nights away together on expenses.

Apart from all that, Karen had told our mutual friends that she'd left me because I was paranoid about her having an affair, probably to make her seem like the victim in all of this and used my mental illness as a tool in justifying her actions – but she was having an affair and so the supposed paranoia wasn't paranoia at all, it was the truth.

I don't know and again it's none of my business, but I'm pretty sure that it may have something to do with him driving a Tesla, buying a half a million love-nest outright, being on a £200K pay scale and her never losing her job because she's secretly doing the boss...it wouldn't surprise me if she's married him before this book even comes out. What I do know, is that Karen could hurt me all she wanted, but when it comes to Sam, then she'd better tread carefully.

It's not a veiled psychopathic threat, I was sectioned for despair not for being murderous, it's just the protective nature of a parent seeing their child in distress. I don't think that in the whirlwind of her not so new romance, Karen had really stopped to think about the impact it was having on Sam. He's twelve going on twenty in terms of physical maturity, but he still has a child's mind that's trying to make sense of the world, as well as having to deal with hormonal changes and having his brain rewired for adulthood.

I don't hate Karen; or Len for that matter, but I don't agree with how she has broached the whole situation with such a lack of understanding for Sam's well-being. ~~~~~~ when it comes to the well-being of my kid. In an almost empathic way, Sam reassured me that I would always be his dad and that Len wouldn't ever take my place and that's when the crack appeared in the dam of emotions that I was trying to hide from him. We sobbed and we hugged, both awash in a tsunami of abandonment, love and confusion and I knew then that I needed to be all that I could for Sam.

Karen still throws the "you're a shit dad because you tried to kill yourself" card at me whenever she is having issues with her own parenting skills, but I don't let it bother me anymore. It was almost like Sam and I had reconnected through the outpouring of grief and we both realised just how important we were to each other...there was never any doubt that I was ever going to be a shit dad, no matter how much of one I felt.

Clue: *despite having difficulties the pain is irreparable*

Say A Little Prayer

Lesley and Arthur have invited Sam and me down to stay with them in Skegness, partly because they're wonderful people and partly because they know that I'm skint and that unscrupulous holiday companies jack up the prices for half-term. I'm a bit nervous about accepting, because it will be my first real outing into the wild, well the wilds of Lincolnshire anyway since becoming independent again. I still have the virtual ankle-tag of having to attend weekly CPN meetings with Shelley and medical check-ups for my toxin levels, but I convince myself that it would be good, if not for myself then for Sam.

Des as accommodating as ever, has offered to drive us the two and a half hours the journey takes by car under the guise of 'having a day out with the missus', so as to not make me feel bad about having to do it on the cheap. I have to pick Sam up en route from my old house and it fills me with dread, having to go back to the place that held so many memories for me. I had to put on my 'game face' despite the sick feeling in my stomach about it being my first separated parent child pick-up, but as soon as I saw Sam's excited grinning face it didn't seem to matter.

The journey down was fairly uneventful, with Sam and Des' daughter syncing up their 'Animal Crossing' avatars on their consoles and keeping each other occupied, whilst Des and Anna sat up front. It gave me the chance to just 'take some time' as I stared out of the window watching the world go by and tried to address the ever growing list of worries and anxieties that I'd built up in my own mind. We eventually arrived and went for a walk along the seafront, before getting something to eat and letting the kids go wild on the tuppence push machines in the amusement arcades.

We said our goodbyes to Des and Anna, before being welcomed by bone-crushingly warm hugs and shown to our rooms by our hosts. The great thing about being at Lesley and Arthur's was that there was no pressure to be involved, take part or even socialise if you didn't feel up to it and I didn't. We were shown where everything we needed was, from snacks to towels and given a set of spare keys for us to come and go as we pleased.

I can't thank them enough for how they made my transition manageable, from being a relative recluse to being able to stroll along a busy promenade full of happy families enjoying the sunshine. It sounds like such a simple thing to do, but when all you have left in the tank are the dregs of a pitiful mix of sludge and despair, it is crippling in every sense of the word. I almost felt like I was in one of those rom-com movies, wherein whatever direction the dejected lover looked, all they saw were scenes of blissful togetherness.

Our week in Skegness together was simple yet amazing...rollercoasters, deep fried Mars Bars, collecting shells, winning toys in the arcades and all shared with the only person that I needed to be here for – Sam. It further reinforced my feeling that ~~[redacted]~~ and it provided a spark to try and rekindle the fire that had dwindled in me. I'd missed him more than I'd realised and seeing him every day this week had reinforced it, but then the darkness crept back in and only added to the fact that these moments would be few and far between once I took him back to Karen.

Clue: *to exist in your absence would be crushing*

Kids

You have to love the brutal honesty of kids. Sam has continuingly been relaying the actions of his mum either from first-hand experience or from what his brother Dean has told him regarding the arrival of Len. Admittedly, I'm a mixture of hurt, anger and delusion both wanting to know and at the same time wanting to be spared the cruelty of loss.

I tell Sam that he doesn't need to tell me anything about his mum, because we're not together anymore, but I get the sense that it's been eating away at him and he has no-one else that he can trust to release his feelings to. I do feel a bit of fatherly pride, that he regards me with such esteem that he's able to do that.

"Okay, you can tell me what's bothering you, but only if you want to." As kids are, there is no gentleness in the turning on of the emotional tap and letting the drops eek out drip by drip, it's an all or nothing flood. Despite having my insides ripped out once again at the replay of our break-up, I listened intently as the pattern of lies and deceit fell into place…

1) The new t-shirt that ended up in my laundry after Karen's latest business trip wasn't one she'd bought in town, it belonged to Len.

2) The extra days Karen stayed away on-site weren't to break up the long drive back, it was to spend time with Len.

3) Karen had only asked me to book and plan our wedding to prompt Len into leaving his wife, for fear of losing her to me – she never intended to go through with the wedding from the start.

4) Whilst on the family holiday in Bulgaria, Karen was constantly messaging Len about how she wished it was him there and not me and left me to occupy Sam.

5) Karen had kept me hanging on as a back-up plan until Len had served his divorce papers to his wife and two kids, in case he didn't have the balls to go through with it. This explains her leaving me at Geoff's that time – I'd obviously touched a nerve in her getting away with it Scott free plan.

There were more such revelations about what I had suspected all along, but I think you get the idea that Karen and Len are both lying, immoral cunts! I confronted Karen about this at a later date, after discovering a parcel with Len's name on it when I dropped Sam off. Apparently, she hadn't been cheating on me, because he was still with his wife at the time...erm, maybe you hadn't fucked him as much by then, but I'm pretty sure that it's still cheating when you're fully aware that each other already have partners.

Sam also told me that Karen slags me off at every opportunity and tells him that I don't do anything to support looking after him, even though I pay for food, clothing, trips etc. It's almost as if she purposefully refuses my extra offers to contribute, in order to slate me for it afterwards and play the martyr. I'm also told that he's overheard her informing anyone she can that I was controlling and turns our split into some kind of domestic violence survivor's story, almost as if her having an affair was some kind of liberation exercise.

I will admit that in the past, some of my obsessive compulsive disorders may have been a bit 'controlling' but there was never any physical or psychological damage to anyone other than myself – my OCD's were rooted in order and symmetry. I would routinely straighten pictures, incessantly tidy up, hang washing out at three in the morning but nothing that would constitute any form of violence – how could I, especially after what I'd witnessed and been subjected to as a child?

I made sure that Sam was okay by making light of the whole thing and passing it off as "Ah well, that's your mum for you!" before I locked myself in the bathroom and tried to push down the feelings of nausea and rage. "▓▓▓▓▓▓▓▓▓▓▓▓▓▓▓▓▓▓▓▓▓▓▓▓▓▓▓▓▓▓▓▓," I told myself. It was a weird feeling; I wasn't upset - because I swore that I would never give Karen the satisfaction again – it was more a sensation of being vindicated about all the doubts and suspicions I'd had, because without trust; there's nothing.

I had done everything that a dutiful, loving fiancée, father and lover should do and there was nothing that the finger of blame could be pointed towards me for. It also made me smile in a kind of 'in your face' way that despite being outwardly pleasant towards Karen and Len in the future, all of our mutual friends that found out Karen had been deceiving them too, would secretly be thinking "You pair of lying, cheating bastards."

I take back that I don't think that Karen was the cause of my attempted suicide – I do, because she was immeasurably cruel. I looked back at my previous attempt in two thousand and twelve and the common theme throughout all of it was Karen. I've been asked by numerous psychiatrist's whether I thought that I was the victim of mental abuse and to be honest - I don't think that I would have recognised the signs - whether through being blinded by love or just being weak.

I don't know, maybe there was some coercion or manipulation there, but that's Len's problem now. If that is the case, then I'm glad that I'm no longer with someone as shallow and deceitful...the look on her face when I told her that I knew all about her catalogue of lies was worth; well about £200K. I've seen pictures of Len and although I'm no stunner, she's not with him for his looks and so it must be his dazzling personality...the schmuck!

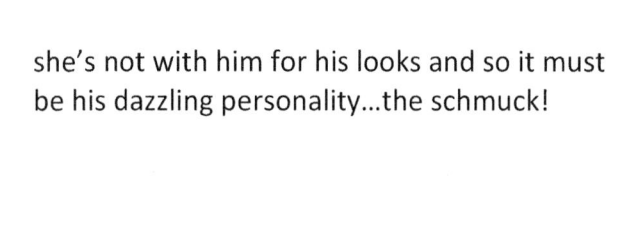

Clue: *use restraint and gain only what's necessary*

Bleed American (Salt, Sweat, Sugar)

I've been in my flat a while now and yet it still seems like a temporary measure rather than a home, almost as if I was still in the halfway house but without the home cooked meals and freely stocked fridge – such comforts are still dictated by motivation and mood. I think in some part; it is because I'm alone except for the weekends that I have Sam or when friends call round for a cuppa on their way through to somewhere else.

I felt so at peace with having the stability of a family home, that now I'm on my own there is nothing to fill the void. No familiar slosh of school uniform in the washing machine, giggles and shrieks from Sam's room as he plays Fortnite with his friends online, no cat purring on my lap as I watch the rain bounce off the window sill, not since I had it all taken away from me.

I have re-arranged furniture, put on my favourite records and hung pictures, all in the hope of creating a familiarity with the space and trying to convince myself that

None of it works of course, because there is something special about what makes a home and the people who you share it with, especially one that you thought you were going to grow old in. I can forgive many things of Karen, but never that she took my home away knowing how hard and how long I'd fought for it, given my family background.

I understand that it is just bricks and mortar, but that's not what she took from me, it was my sense of belonging. I had finally found somewhere that wasn't transient, where I didn't feel out of place or saw as a stop-gap and I'd put every fibre of my being in to. It was more than a house, it was somewhere I called home in a world that I didn't feel part of and it was full of the people that I loved.

I loved being on the road or in transit, most likely because of all my years of running from my past. So, the sheer fact that I had a spot that didn't make me feel like I needed to be someplace else, was testament to its importance for me and although my little one bedroomed flat is great, it's not a home.

I am eternally grateful to my support worker Anne for managing to find me somewhere that allowed me easy access to Sam's school run, not a million miles away from being able to see him and not in some damp, rough arse tower block that I was more than likely destined to throw myself off rather than end up in.

It's a weird contradictory system that the social housing model is built on and I was way down the waiting list, when the flat I eventually got came onto the market. I wasn't able to access the online portal that the housing listings are uploaded to, partly because I wasn't technically eligible due to being an in-patient (you don't count if you're somebody else's problem) and partly because of the crappy Wi-Fi and so I was reliant on Anne to place bids for me.

A bid is exactly as it sounds, in that you have to throw your hat into the ring to even be considered and even then, if you make it to the top of the list there's no guarantee that you will get the property...you literally might as well bet it all on black and hope for the best.

Despite making it to the top of the list once the bidding has ended, there's then the process of verifying eligibility, circumstance and banding. Each local authority has its own version of the banding process, some use numbers, some letters and some colours i.e. gold, silver, bronze and so there's no universal system and I've been assured that if you're anywhere past number five, D or bronze on the list, then forget it for the next three years, if ever. I, because Sam would be spending some, if not all of the week with me when Karen was 'working' on-site with her boss Len, was an influencing factor and so I was put in to the Silver category.

Still no dice however; Silver was obviously better than the infinity of Bronze, but I was still way off getting anywhere and my email sign-ups to the local letting agents hadn't yielded anything other than places with rents that equalled Liberia's national deficit with an equally poor standard of dwelling. Given the monumental efforts that Anne had been putting in, it ultimately came down to a stroke of luck and believe it or not for the first time ever, my age was on my side. At the end of the bidding process, I had finished eighth on the list and had resided myself to the fact that I wasn't going anywhere soon, but in some karmic twist of fate I won...maybe all that free ward work did pay off after all.

It turned out that due to a combination of where the flat was, in a small unit of six, its inhabitants all being in the forty plus age category and all of the winning bidders before me taking other properties (you can bid on multiple ones at once) that I ended up being the only one with any eligibility left. It doesn't end there though, because there is then a long winded process of the 'empty homes' team who go in to assess what state the previous tenant has left the place in. From what I gather, this basically entails contractors spinning out the days on site to charge the local authority more for tidying up the place and it was another six weeks before I eventually got the keys.

I am truly fortunate and thankful for having such a great place to live and I don't care that the walls are thin enough to hear what my neighbours are watching on TV – it's safe, it's clean and it's mine for as long as I need it. Yeah, it kills my back when I sleep on the couch because I've given Sam the only bedroom, so that he has his own space when he's here. Yes, I miss having a garden and watching my beehive at work in the long Summer months. So, I don't have enough space to keep a shed's worth possessions, but then again they still wouldn't make it feel like home.

Clue: *not solo due to the idiot box*

Caught In A Mosh

My ventures into social situations is still pretty limited, partly because I don't feel comfortable being around people that I know and partly because I don't have the strength to fight back the trauma of what I'd done, trying to tell the same story over and over again. I do miss live music though – if playing a record is sitting around with your vinyl friends, then a live gig is partying with them. Knowing how much I need to just get lost in something familiar, Geoff gets us tickets to an Anthrax 40th Anniversary gig in Leeds and I have enough forewarning to both fret about it and psyche myself up in readiness.

The day finally arrives and although I'm still bricking it, I go to catch the train and like some omen of foreboding it gets cancelled, I don't know why I'm surprised at this revelation that the rail network in the U.K. sucks, but there you go. I eventually arrive and in true Geoff fashion, he is also late and so I stand in the bustle of the foyer in a ▓▓▓▓▓▓▓▓▓▓▓▓ ▓▓▓▓▓▓ open and shut in a nervous panic about being somehow exposed in a crowd. It is ridiculous, seeing as I've agreed to be part of a sold out show and yet without the comfort blanket of music around me, I somehow feel naked.

When Geoff finally arrives, we head to the bar next to the venue, because neither of us are particularly fussed about the support band, having seen them before and thinking that they were, well...just a bit meh. I limit myself to two drinks given the advice of the doctors that my liver had taken a battering from the Paracetamol and stay to the fringes of social groups and conversations.

The bar is rammed like nineteen eighty-six had time warped everyone from that era to this exact spot, with the only difference being that we were all just a little bit older, fatter and balder. The conversations that I am dragged into mainly consist of what I've been doing since the last one of these tribal gatherings, to which I generically reply with some sort of 'this and that' response. I ask Geoff if we can head inside, feeling the pressure of having to come up with topics of conversation or to elaborate on my vague answers and he agrees.

Once in the venue with it's throng of voices and P.A. decibels pumping out while the stage crew frantically change over set, I immediately feel calmer. I truly believe in the power of music as a healer for everything from heartbreak and loneliness to death and resurrection and it's no surprise that seeing Anthrax would transport me back to a time when I felt alive.

For those of you not well versed in the thrash metal scene of the eighties, Anthrax were part of what was known as the 'Big Four' bands of that time (Metallica, Megadeth, Slayer, Anthrax). It was a different feeling being in a gig crowd as opposed to the train station or bar - I couldn't be part of a conversation, nobody knew who I was and more importantly I was immersed in sound - I lost Geoff to the mosh-pit within the first two songs.

Clue: *icy perspiration, balled hands*

Bad Liver & A Broken Heart

I've just had my three monthly 'you tried to kill yourself' physical review (the mental is weekly) and it turns out that the doctors initial concern that I'd done a proper number on my liver was on the money. The good news is that it's not going to kill me (bugger), but I've increased a few factors that could and it's definite that I won't be getting a birthday telegram from the king for sure. I'm amazed that I had a healthy liver at all, given the years of hard drinking and that a simple hangover paracetamol in excessive amounts is the thing that's fucked me up.

Liver fibrosis is essentially scarring of the organ, which eventually builds to cirrhosis over time as the nodules harden. I'm at the compensated cirrhosis stage, which means that my liver is scarred but coping with daily functions, despite the damage caused by the toxin levels of my overdose. The next steps are to run further tests and maybe put me on lipophilic statins, due to the liver not being able to regulate my cholesterol levels properly, which therefore increases the risks of things like heart disease or stroke.

I scored pretty well on the 'how soon you're going to need a transplant and/or die' scales, so I'm just going to have to make lifestyle changes i.e. low sodium, not getting hammered and so on. I doubt that I'd accept a transplant anyway, because my issues are self-inflicted and there are others in the world that just never had a choice and to me, it would seem unfair to use the opportunity.

I guess that's why I'm okay just to keep nursing my ~~██████████████████████~~, because I did it to myself and for me it's a win/win...like a bonus 'get out' clause without the guilt. I'll probably live for ages now in a "Ha ha...you're fucked but you ain't getting off that easy" way that life often uses to taunt you. I'm not concerned – I mean...any of us could get hit by a bus tomorrow and then having a dodgy liver wouldn't have made any difference now would it?

Clue: *not good internal organs*

Many Of Horror

So, here I am ~~redacted~~ ~~redacted~~ in the hope that I make it through another year without the magic of Metuzar to help me. I never thought that I'd make it past thirty and view the extra twenty years I've had, as some strange combination of luck and penance. Yes...of course I am blessed with the miracle of having healthy, beautiful and loving sons; even though I don't think I count for much, if anything with Dean anymore – I didn't even get a card for my 50th. I still take the pills, try to exercise regularly and check in with my care worker at weekly intervals and still none of it seems to matter – my mind seems intent on me just existing and not living and it's not through lack of trying on my part.

I've tried to focus my attentions on being more positive and productive by writing this book, being outdoors and working as a volunteer with the mental health charity Healthy Minds; by drawing on my teaching experience and facilitating workshops that work with eight to nineteen year olds to promote mental wellbeing – something I never had, but probably needed in the days of 'just get on with it and stop being soft' when I was at school. I am still for all intents and purposes 'living a lie' and don't practice what I preach, but I never have been the main focus of anything that I do for a very long time, if ever.

I do believe in what I'm doing with the young adults and I am fully committed to providing them with a better understanding of what mental health can look like from a personal and professional perspective, but I gain no sense of self-worth or meaningfulness from it. Do I practice altruism to an extreme form of selflessness, or is it that I'm seeking ways to validate my existence?

Maybe that's what life should be about, selfless pursuits and not 'what's in it for me?' unlike most of the billionaire one percent seem to base their self-worth on – I mean; you never see a poor elitist begging for change, so maybe that's the type of society we've become. If you are self-absorbed, when does it stop being focussed self-care and start being selfish abandon?

I guess that it just comes down to the multitude of factors that we are subjected to from parents, siblings and society as a whole that ultimately determines how we might turn out as well as some hardwiring. In some ways my own pessimistic outlook of seeing yourself as being at the bottom and therefore unable to get any lower, itself gives rise to the optimism of the only way being up as a back-handed armchair philosophy.

No-one has all the answers and even with Gilligan's eyes of naïve optimism along with the eye of the idol (that one's for you Simon Neil), he ultimately ends up being marooned back on the same island again in the end. To some extent, it can be viewed as you getting dealt a pontoon hand that no matter how many times you twist, you never beat the banker...and maybe that's just life.

My friend Jamie always tells me that, "If he didn't have bad luck, he'd have no luck at all" and so any type of luck is better than nothing – a real 'turn that frown upside down' way of looking at the world.

So, where to next on my journey of self-care? Ugh...I hate that terminology – it sounds like having a wank in soft focus, but it does make sense for someone who doesn't really value much about themselves.

The honest answer is that I don't know...I still wake up with the same emptiness every day, the low self-worth, the lack of joy in anything other than when I have Sam for the weekends and even then it's all about him and not me. I don't know how much longer I'll be able to hold out, but I'm taking each day as it comes and I fight the dark as best I can – it's draining, but I've made it this far.

I really hope that I haven't come across as some kind of woman hater in this book - I don't hate anyone because it's a massive waste of time and energy, despite what's happened to me. There are always multiple sides to every story; I'm just hurting and so I wrote mine down – I still find it strange that some people value money over true love though.

I've learned that it's okay to not get on with everyone, as long as you're not the one causing distress and that the people who project their own lack of compassion on to others, are to be educated rather than despised. The world as it stands is broken, none more so than Britain, which isn't doing anyone's head any good but the next generation of protesters, activists and campaigners have a fighting chance to fix it, if we all act in the best interests of the many rather than the few.

I've just realised that this section is turning into a rallying cry for the socialist movement, but where's the harm in wanting a fairer society? I'm glad that a greater awareness of mental health is becoming more mainstream and that more and more people are embracing being open about what does their noodle in.

If we're mindful of others and guide with acceptance rather than prejudice to create a more caring environment, then we can alleviate some of the everyday pressures that mess with our minds – rattling pots and pans on a Thursday night never saved anyone, but a simple hello to a stranger at a bus stop just might.

We don't know our own minds most of the time and science has a better understanding about the depths of space and the bottom of the oceans, as opposed to the human brain and so until it does, it's up to us both as individuals and collectively to work it out and hold each other up now and again. If there's anything that I want you the reader to take away from this book, it's that there is always hope no matter how desperate the situation might seem.

Be kind, check in on those you cherish - especially the ones who laugh the loudest, because they're most likely drowning on the inside. Fill each day like it could be your last, be sure that you don't harm others, choose love over hate, but most of all...live!

[cue Iggy Pop soundtrack]
Duh duh duh, da da da duh da da...~~~~~~~~~~!

Clue 1: *resting in a well, praying for sun*

Clue 2: *desire for living*

Hidden Bonus Track - Arlandria

I've obviously taken you on a journey through my continuing recovery and so it seems only fitting to leave you with the former suicide note, that nearly became the end of my journey.

It's been quite difficult to re-read for myself, especially knowing how much of a bitch Karen really is now. If you; like I did, think that all the stuff like wills, funerals, inheritance etc. is far too grown up to worry about yet, then get your shit together and put things in place…but then again ~~the shit else matter, watch it all go up in flames~~ (literally).

Clue: *it's no different, observe it on fire*

Karen: My heart is broken. I'd finally found peace with myself and was looking forward to a future for the first time. There is no one else that I wanted to spend the rest of my days with and I'd done everything that you've ever asked of me to ensure that. All I had ever wanted was to feel 'home' and have a family around me that I cherished and with you I had it, which is part of the reason I always wanted to be in our space. I understand that it was hard for you, given my mental state and you struggling with the menopause...I don't blame you for any of this. You always said that you didn't need me, but I couldn't bear that you didn't want me and I'm sorry that I never realised that you were just as damaged as I was.

I guess I've left you in the same situation as when we met, with everything still on your terms but hopefully a bit better off. I didn't get a say in whether we stayed together, stayed in our bedroom or in our home – I don't know if you ever really loved me; or whether I was just a convenient option to make your life a bit easier. I've tried to take care of everything that I could think of and hope that you have finally got who and what you feel you need – you always got your own way in the end anyway.

The funeral is all paid for, so you just have to arrange when – I didn't use the £500 bank transfer, so the £10K I gave you should cover my share of the mortgage for the next year and to take you and the boys away for a holiday. Please know that I never stopped loving you and that there wasn't a day that I wasn't thankful, for every time you kept me steady.

Dean: I know that we had a difficult start, but I want you to know that I am so proud of the person that you have become. I was glad to be your dad and felt like we'd finally found common ground, especially during our last holiday. Your brother is going to need you to guide him and be there, now that I'm not. Although there haven't been enough case studies, there is the possibility that Dysthymia can be 'inherited' in children (DSM-III), so keep an eye on him once the pubescent hormones have settled down. You're an amazing son and brother and I know that your mum and Sam will be just fine with you around.

Sam: You are the greatest thing that has ever happened to me in my whole life. I have watched you grow into a kind, caring, loving young man and I am so proud to have been there to see it. You are amazing and can do anything you set your mind to and I'm sure that you'll do great things in the future. You are so grown up now, that you can handle anything that life will throw at you with courage, determination and a great group of family and friends. I never want you to ever feel as alone as I did – and you won't, because you've got a brilliant mum and an awesome brother. I will never stop loving you and you will always be my everything – write me a story one day, like the ones I used to tell you...I love you Doodles!

Funeral:

████████████████████ package which has already been paid in full, including all legal fees, certificates etc. The contact is: ████████ ██████████████████████████████ and the contract includes: Funeral Directors services, collection of deceased during office hours, care of deceased prior to Cremation, choice of Crematorium, simple coffin, transportation in suitable vehicle, attendance at crematorium, service time agreed with family, choice of readings and music, special requests such as dress code, provision of cremated remains,

Doctors' fees included, Cremation fees guaranteed, nationwide collection (there is no mileage restriction) - the documentation is with the rest of my effects.

Service:
The date and time of the service at ▮▮▮▮▮ just needs to be arranged. There is no additional cost, so you just need to turn up on the day – everything else is done. I have already compiled the service booklet, which has been mailed to Jim to be printed. All the eulogies etc. and names of orators are listed inside it. I have made Geoff the 'legacy' contact on Facebook to post details of the service. My mum's number is: ▮▮▮▮▮ – she can come, but may need wheelchair transport arranging...again; there is enough money to cover it.

Last Will & Testament:
The Will was updated on 18th June 2022 which supersedes the earlier version held at ▮▮▮▮▮. In addition to this, there is a list of personal chattels that I would like to bequest, detailed within the pages of the Will for either keepsakes or to be auctioned. Any monies

gained from the sale of such items should be distributed between ▮▮▮▮▮▮▮▮▮▮ and a donation made to the mental health charity ▮▮▮▮▮▮. There is no need for a solicitor to be involved because it is a straightforward and detailed Codicil to my original Will made on 17th December 2012, when I last planned to take my own life.

Crematorium Service:
[Entry music: I Started A Joke – Faith No More version]

Jim: Johnny as you knew, liked doing things his way to the point where he's even written my part. So, anything that comes out of my mouth now, are his words and you can take it up with him afterwards. He wanted Des to know that he would have asked him to also speak, but he knows how shit he is at social situations.

I won't go on about how kind, caring and how much of a great friend he was, because if you're here then you know all that stuff already. Instead, he wanted me to talk about some of the reasons 'why' he did what he did, in the hope that it will help you understand.

Johnny's mind had always been troubled – it was just wired wrong from day one. Yeah, there were factors that would have been influencing forces, but it's not a sob-story. He had done some cool shit in his time, met some great people along the way and settled down with Karen and his kids Dean and Sam.

Most people have heard about the 'black dog' syndrome - Johnny had an entire rescue centre's worth of canines that never left his mind quiet. The official diagnosis was Dysthymia or Persistent Depressive Disorder, but Johnny never thought he was depressed – he liked to think of it more as not being able to handle life...depression didn't kill him, a broken heart did.

He left us because of what it was doing to those he loved and after forty plus years, he couldn't see an end in sight. When your 'black dog' starts affecting your partner and children, even though you've tried all the psychobabble and pill popping to muzzle it, the only option he felt he had left, was to put it down. You may consider it cowardly, an easy way out or selfish and maybe you're right, but the Johnny I knew was selfless.

Please join me in a song dedicated to Sam and Dean.
[Father & Son – Cat Stevens]

Geoff: As a lot of you know, Johnny loved playing drums, being outdoors and going to gigs. It was great until he started physically falling to pieces, as well as mentally. He developed a degenerative bone disease in his spine, first starting with nerve damage in his neck, before affecting his lumbar and causing osteoarthritis to the point of continually being in pain. He would always say that the stagediving, lugging amps and gigging were worth it and he wouldn't have changed a thing.

Eventually though, it began to affect his quality of life which added to his mental state – we're all getting on a bit, but even simple tasks started becoming frustrating for him. I know I could talk about the fun times, but as Johnny informed me, "I've only paid for twenty minutes coffin parking, gerron wi it - I am a Yorkshireman after all!"

Gordooooom: Following on from Geoff; Johnny wanted to clarify that he completely understood why Karen couldn't cope being his emotional crutch any longer. When your mind is erratic and pulled in different directions, things like how it affects others aren't always obvious. Karen had already felt the effects of sitting in A&E with the crisis team, psychologists and home visits to make sure he took his medication over the years, so it's not surprising that it eventually broke her and the kids.

He wants Karen, Dean and Sam to know that none of this is their fault and that they or anyone else shouldn't feel like it was because of something they did. Johnny had an illness – one that you rarely saw unless you really knew him and because he was always concerned with making everyone else happy, it never truly showed itself. Save the stories of the good times for when he's listening, although he never remembered to put his hearing aids in anyway!

Please join me in our final song which is dedicated to Karen.
[Who Knew? – P!nk]

[Exit music: Black – Pearl Jam MTV Unplugged version]

Obituary:
Johnny Cashback
███████

Beloved father, teacher, musician.
"For those about to rock, we salute you!"

What is Dysthymia (PDD)

Persistent depressive disorder symptoms usually come and go over a period of years, and their intensity can change over time, but typically symptoms don't disappear for more than two months at a time. In addition, major depression episodes may occur before or during persistent depressive disorder — this is sometimes called double depression.

Symptoms of persistent depressive disorder can cause significant impairment and may include:

- Loss of interest in daily activities
- Sadness, emptiness or feeling down
- Hopelessness
- Tiredness and lack of energy
- Low self-esteem, self-criticism or feeling incapable
- Trouble concentrating and trouble making decisions

- Irritability or excessive anger

- Decreased activity, effectiveness and productivity

- Avoidance of social activities

- Feelings of guilt and worries over the past
- Poor appetite or overeating

- Sleep problems

- In children, symptoms of persistent depressive disorder may include depressed mood and irritability.

For partners of those with mental health issues:
www.mentalhealthforum.net

For children with mental health issues:
www.youngminds.org.uk

For those with mental health issues:
www.nhs.uk

Quotes from my friends when I asked them to give this book a read through... and this is why I love them!

"It's a bit wanky in parts." – Ceri

"Dude...no way, that's awesome!" – Des

ہم اب بھی تم سے نفرت کرتے ہیں گورا
– my Asian relatives

"Wonderfully, heartbreakingly real." – Sarah H.

"Is leathcheann thú ach is breá liom tú!"
– Helen

"We'll see you in court!" – Karen and Len

Guess The Lyrics Game

Song: Where Is My Mind?
Artist: The Pixies
Clue: far out at sea you can observe the backstroke
Words: 8

Song: Suffragette City
Artist: David Bowie
Clue: being leant on and not having enough funds to pay the fine
Words: 11

Song: Hotel California
Artist: The Eagles
Clue: something about being able to go, but inevitably being stuck there
Words: 11

Song: Help!
Artist: The Beatles
Clue: S.O.S. request
Words: 1

Song: Screamager
Artist: Therapy?
Clue: being bored without a release
Words: 11

Song: Comfortably Numb
Artist: Pink Floyd
Clue: being pleasantly unable to feel
Words: 5

Song: If It Makes You Happy
Artist: Sheryl Crow
Clue: wearing an item of clothing, performing for insects until needing a drink
Words: 15

Song: Hedonism (Just Because You Feel Good)
Artist: Skunk Anansie
Clue: deriving pleasure might still not deem it acceptable
Words: 9

Song: What I've Done
Artist: Linkin Park
Clue: rubbing out oneself
Words: 10

Song: We Have All The Time In The World
Artist: Louis Armstrong
Clue: an abundance of free time
Words: 6

Song: The Day I Tried To Live
Artist: Soundgarden
Clue: not meeting your own expectations
Words: 11

Song: Who Knew?
Artist: P!nk
Clue: eternally wondering
Words: 5

Song: Simple Man
Artist: Lynard Skynard
Clue: fret not, use your soul, be confident, my wish is for your contentment
Words: 39

Song: Battery
Artist: Metallica
Clue: multiple power cells
Words: 1

Song: Save Myself
Artist: Ed Sheeran
Clue: stuck amidst evil and peril
Words: 9

Song: The Lost Art Of Keeping A Secret
Artist: Queens Of The Stone Age
Clue: please don't inform others
Words: 6

Song: Don't Get Me Wrong
Artist: The Pretenders
Clue: don't misunderstand me
Words: 4

Song: Disciple
Artist: Slayer
Clue: a higher power dislikes us
Words: 4

Song: Livin' On The Edge
Artist: Aerosmith
Clue: can you explain your predicament
Words: 8

Song: Smoke 'Em
Artist: Fun Lovin' Criminals
Clue: use the items if you have them in your possession
Words: 17

Song: You Can't Always Get What You Want
Artist: The Rolling Stones
Clue: you may not be able to fulfil your needs
Words: 7

Song: Jigsaw Puzzle
Artist: The Rolling Stones
Clue: attempting to complete a task before the weather changes
Words: 12

Song: The Man Who Sold The World
Artist: David Bowie
Clue: claimed that I was a companion, eliciting a revelation
Words: 11

Song: Only Happy When It Rains
Artist: Garbage
Clue: deriving joy from sadness
Words: 5

Song: Orange Tree Roads
Artist: New Model Army
Clue: stood in daylight in crops of wheat
Words: 9

Song: Bringin' On The Heartbreak
Artist: Def Leppard
Clue: apologetically, the fact is that you are causing distress
Words: 10

Song: Sweet Soul Sister
Artist: The Cult
Clue: time tricks those nearing death
Words: 7

Song: State Of Love & Trust
Artist: Pearl Jam
Clue: being attentive to inner thoughts
Words: 7

Song: The Drug's Don't Work
Artist: The Verve
Clue: a feline awaiting an imminent watery death
Words: 9

Song: Wandering Star
Artist: Portishead
Clue: internally folded whilst being upset
Words: 10

Song: Check My Brain
Artist: Alice In Chains
Clue: weeping saturates skeletal form
Words: 5

Song: Chop Suey
Artist: System Of A Down
Clue: is there a reason to abandon me?
Words: 5

Song: Nearly Lost You
Artist: Screaming Trees
Clue: a faraway call asking me to return
Words: 9

Song: Heaven Knows I'm Miserable Now
Artist: The Smiths
Clue: pleasantly inebriated for sixty minutes
Words: 10

Song: Streets Of Philadelphia
Artist: Bruce Springsteen
Clue: unable to comprehend due to injuries
Words: 11

Song: Mr. Jones
Artist: Counting Crows
Clue: produce art using a range of colours
Words: 15

Song: Ode To My Family
Artist: The Cranberries
Clue: am I visible or even valued?
Words: 7

Song: Big Gay Heart
Artist: The Lemonheads
Clue: over a period of time the pain may alleviate
Words: 11

Song: Don't Believe A Word
Artist: Thin Lizzy
Clue: what I say may be false or not
Words: 14

Song: Wanted Dead Or Alive
Artist: Bon Jovi
Clue: witnessed a multitude of likenesses
Words: 3

Song: Wasted Years
Artist: Iron Maiden
Clue: not knowing oneself or one's actions
Words: 18

Song: Self-Esteem
Artist: The Offspring
Clue: suffrage equates to displays of loving
Words: 12

Song: Low Self Opinion
Artist: Rollins Band
Clue: awareness of mental emotions
Words: 10

Song: Bullet With Butterfly Wings
Artist: Smashing Pumpkins
Clue: I'm a prisoner regardless of my feelings
Words: 12

Song: Accidents Can Happen
Artist: Sixx AM
Clue: not your whole existence, just a part of it
Words: 9

Song: Psycho Killer
Artist: Talking Heads
Clue: my anxiety makes it difficult to be calm
Words: 8

Song: Stand Up
Artist: Thunder
Clue: periodically you may blemish
Words: 4

Song: Don't Let Me Be Misunderstood
Artist: Nina Simone
Clue: my erratic demeanour wasn't directed at you
Words: 19

Song: Adam's Song
Artist: Blink 182
Clue: I never imagined death in solitude
Words: 6

Song: Don't Shit Where You Eat
Artist: Ween
Clue: refrain from defecating near food
Words: 7

Song: Fisherman's Blues
Artist: The Waterboys
Clue: brightness of mind, one held close
Words: 7

Song: Outside/Inside
Artist: The Levellers
Clue: not inside through no fault of their own
Words: 10

Song: Waking Up
Artist: Elastica
Clue: prepare a beverage, play some vinyl
Words: 9

Song: 9 to 5
Artist: Dolly Parton
Clue: a means to earn a wage
Words: 7

Song: Last Christmas
Artist: Wham
Clue: she ripped to pieces
Words: 4

Song: King Of The Whole Wide World
Artist: Elvis Presley
Clue: a male who vocalises despite having nought, is the ruler of the globe
Words: 20

Song: Lucille
Artist: Kenny Rogers
Clue: despite having difficulties the pain is irreparable
Words: 17

Song: Say A Little Prayer
Artist: Aretha Franklin
Clue: to exist in your absence would be crushing
Words: 10

Song: Kids
Artist: MGMT
Clue: use restraint and gain only what's necessary
Words: 10

Song: Bleed American (Salt, Sweat, Sugar)
Artist: Jimmy Eat World
Clue: not solo due to the idiot box
Words: 7

Song: Caught In A Mosh
Artist: Anthrax
Clue: icy perspiration, balled hands
Words: 5

Song: Bad Liver & A Broken Heart
Artist: Scott Nolan
Clue: not good internal organs
Words: 5

Song: Many Of Horror
Artist: Biffy Clyro
Clue: resting in a well, praying for sun
Words: 9

Song: Lust For Life
Artist: Iggy Pop
Clue: desire for living
Words: 3

Song: Arlandria
Artist: Foo Fighters
Clue: it's no different, observe it on fire
Words: 11

Discography

Where Is My Mind? – The Pixies
(1988 Thompson)

Suffragette City – David Bowie
(1972 Bowie)

Morning Mood – Edvard Grieg
(1875 Grieg)

Hotel California – The Eagles
(1977 Felder/Henley/Frey)

Help! – The Beatles
(1965 Lennon/McCartney)

One Flew Over The Cuckoo's Nest – Theme
(1975 Nitzsche)

Russians – Sting
(1985 Sting/Prokofiev)

Screamager – Therapy?
(1994 Cairns/Ewing/McKeegan)

Comfortably Numb – Pink Floyd
(1980 Gilmour/Waters)

If It Makes You Happy – Sheryl Crow
(1996 Crow/Trott)

Hedonism (Just Because You Feel Good) –
Skunk Anansie
(1996 Skin/Arran)

What I've Done – Linkin Park
(2007 Bennington/Hahn/Bourdon/Delson/
Farrell/Shinoda)

We Have All The Time In The World – Louis
Armstrong
(1969 David/Barry)

The Day I Tried To Live – Soundgarden
(1994 Cornell)

Who Knew? – P!nk
(2006 Moore/Martin/Gottwald)

Simple Man – Lynard Skynard
(1973 Van Zant/Rossington)

Battery – Metallica
(1986 Hetfield/Burton/Ulrich)

Save Myself – Ed Sheeran
(2017 Sheeran/Wadge/Labrinth)

The Lost Art Of Keeping A Secret – Queens Of The Stone Age
(2000 Homme/Oliveri)

Don't Get Me Wrong – The Pretenders
(1986 Hynde)

How Great Thou Art – Stuart K. Hine
(1885 Boberg)

King Of Kings, Lord of Lords – Marantha
(1980 Batya/Conty)

Disciple – Slayer
(2001 King/Hanneman)

Livin' On The Edge - Aerosmith
(1993 Hudson/Tyler/Perry)

Smoke 'Em – Fun Lovin' Criminals
(1996 Leiser/Morgan/Borgovini)

Paint It Black – The Rolling Stones
(1966 Jagger/Richards)

Mother's Little Helper – The Rolling Stones
(1966 Jagger/Richards)

19th Nervous Breakdown – The Rolling Stones
(1966 Jagger/Richards)

You Can't Always Get What You Want – The Rolling Stones
(1969 Jagger/Richards)

Jigsaw Puzzle – The Rolling Stones
(1968 Jagger/Richards)

The Man Who Sold The World – David Bowie
(1970 Bowie)

Only Happy When It Rains – Garbage
(1995 Erikson/Manson/Marker/Vig)

Toast – Street Band
(1978 Kelly)

Orange Tree Roads – New Model Army
(2000 Sullivan)

Bringin' On The Heartbreak – Def Leppard
(1981 Clark/Willis/Elliot)

Sweet Soul Sister – The Cult
(1989 Duffy/Astbury)

State Of Love & Trust – Pearl Jam
(1992 Vedder/Ament/McCready)

The Drug's Don't Work – The Verve
(1997 Ashcroft)

Wandering Star – Portishead
(1994 Gibbons/Barrow)

Check My Brain – Alice In Chains
(2009 Cantrell)

Chop Suey – System Of A Down
(2001 Malakian/Tankian)

Nearly Lost You – Screaming Trees
(1992 Lanegan/Conner/Conner)

Heaven Knows I'm Miserable Now – The Smiths
(1984 (Morrissey/Marr)

There's A Light That Never Goes Out – The Smiths
(1985 Morrissey/Marr)

How Soon Is Now? – The Smiths
(1985 Morrissey/Marr)

Streets Of Philadelphia – Bruce Springsteen
(1993 Springsteen)

Mr. Jones - Counting Crows
(1993 Bryson/Duritz)

Ode To My Family – The Cranberries
(1994 O'Riordan/Hogan)

Big Gay Heart – The Lemonheads
(1993 Dando/Morgan)

Don't Believe A Word – Thin Lizzy
(1976 Lynott)

The Old Rugged Cross – George Bennard
(1912 Bennard)

Wanted Dead Or Alive – Bon Jovi
(1987 Bon Jovi/Sambora)

Wasted Years – Iron Maiden
(1986 Smith)

Self-Esteem – The Offspring
(1994 Holland)

Low Self Opinion - Rollins Band
(1992 Rollins/Cain/Haskett/Weiss)

Bullet With Butterfly Wings – Smashing Pumpkins
(1995 Corgan)

Accidents Can Happen – Sixx A.M.
(2007 Sixx/Ashba/Michael)

Psycho Killer – Talking Heads
(1977 Byrne/Weymouth/Frantz)

Stand Up – Thunder
(1995 Bowes)

Don't Let Me Be Misunderstood – Nina Simone
(1965 Benjamin/Ott/Marcus)

Adam's Song – Blink 182
(1999 Hoppus/Barker/DeLonge)

Don't Shit Where You Eat – Ween
(1994 D. Ween/G. Ween)

Fisherman's Blues – The Waterboys
(1998 Wickham/Scott)

Outside/Inside – The Levellers
(1990 Chadwick/Cunningham/Sevink/Heather/Miles)

Waking Up – Elastica
(1995 Frischmann)

9 to 5 – Dolly Parton
(1980 Parton)

Last Christmas – Wham
(1984 Michael)

King Of The Whole Wide World – Elvis Presley
(1962 Batchelor/Roberts)

Lucille – Kenny Rogers
(1977 Bynum/Bowling)

Say A Little Prayer – Aretha Franklin
(1968 Bacharach/David)

Kids – MGMT
(2007 Goldwasser/ Van Wyngarden)

Bleed American (Salt, Sweat, Sugar) – Jimmy Eat World
(2001 Adkins/Burch/Lind/Linton)

Caught In A Mosh – Anthrax
(1987 Belladonna/Ian/Banante/Bello/Spitz)

Bad Liver & A Broken Heart – Scott Nolan
(2008 Nolan)

Many Of Horror – Biffy Clyro
(2009 Neil)

Lust For Life – Iggy Pop
(1977 Pop/Bowie)

Arlandria – Foo Fighters
(2011 Grohl/Hawkins/Mendel/Shiflett/Smear)

I Started A Joke – Faith No More
(1968 B. Gibb/R. Gibb/M.Gibb)

Father And Son – Cat Stevens
(1970 Stevens)

Black – Pearl Jam
(1991 Gossard)

References

ADHD: Attention Deficit Hyperactivity Disorder is a condition that affects people's behaviour.
Source: www.nhs.uk/conditions/attention-deficit-hyperactivity-disorder-adhd

Adjustment Disorder: adjustment disorders are stress-related conditions. You experience more stress than would normally be expected in response to a stressful or unexpected event, and the stress causes significant problems in your relationships, at work or at school.

Adjustment disorders affect how you feel and think about yourself and the world and may also affect your actions or behaviour.
Source: www.mayoclinic.org/diseases-conditions/adjustment-disorders/symptoms-causes/syc-20355224

Adventure Time: formerly known as Adventure Time with Finn and Jake was an American animated television series created by Pendleton Ward and produced by Frederator Studios.
Source: https://adventuretime.fandom.com/wiki/Adventure_Time

Andy's Man Club: are a men's suicide prevention charity, offering free-to-attend peer-to-peer support groups across the United Kingdom and online.
Source: https://andysmanclub.co.uk

Animal Crossing: is a social simulation video game series developed and published by Nintendo.
Source: https://animal-crossing.com

Animal Farm: is a commentary on the development of Russian communism under Joseph Stalin (1878–1953) delivered in allegorical form by author George Orwell.
Source: https://www.bl.uk/works/animal-farm

Anthrax: is an American heavy metal band from New York City formed in 1981.
Source: https://www.anthrax.com

Anxiety: There are several types of anxiety disorders, including generalized anxiety disorder, panic disorder, social anxiety disorder, and various phobia-related disorders.
Source: www.nimh.nih.gov/health/ topics/ anxiety-disorders

Apis: was an ancient, Egyptian bull god of fertility and the underworld.
Source: https://study.com/academy/lesson/ apis-egyptian-god-facts-symbolism.html

Ayatollah Khomeini: Khomeini was an Iranian religious and political leader, who in 1979 made Iran the world's first recognised Islamic republic.
Source: https://www.bbc.co.uk/history/historic _figures/khomeini_ayatollah.shtml

Beatles: were an English rock band, formed in Liverpool in 1960, that comprised John Lennon, Paul McCartney, George Harrison and Ringo Starr.
Source: www//en.wikipedia.org/wiki/ The_Beatles

Big Issue: the UK's number one street paper and social enterprise, giving people who are experiencing homelessness or who are vulnerably housed a hand up.
Source: www.bigissue.com

Blair Cunningham: is an American drummer who has played for many bands and artists.
Source: https://www.discogs.com/artist/ 266077-Blair-Cunningham

Bodil Joensen: was a Danish pornographic actress born in the village of Hundige, near Copenhagen.
Source: https://en.wikipedia.org/wiki / Bodil_Joensen

Brave New World: a dystopian novel by English author Aldous Huxley, written in 1931 and set in a futuristic World State, inhabited by genetically modified citizens and an intelligence-based social hierarchy.
Source: www.goodreads.com/book/show/5129.Brave_New_World

Cadbury: formerly Cadbury's and Cadbury Schweppes, is a British multinational confectionery company owned by Mondelez International since 2010. It is the second largest confectionery brand in the world after Mars.
Source: https://en.wikipedia.org/wiki/Cadbury

Canadian Caper: the joint covert rescue by the Canadian government and the CIA of six American diplomats who had evaded capture during the seizure of the United States embassy in Tehran on 4th November 1979 after the Iranian Revolution.
Source: https://en.wikipedia.org/wiki/Canadian_Caper

Carl Jung: was a Swiss psychologist and psychiatrist who founded analytic psychology. Jung proposed and developed the concepts of the extraverted and the introverted personality, archetypes, and the collective unconscious.
Source: www.britannica.com/biography/Carl-Jung

Charles Manson: was an American cult leader whose followers carried out several notorious murders in the late 1960s, resulting in his life imprisonment.
Source: https://www.biography.com/crime/charles-manson

CND: Campaign For Nuclear Disarmament (CND) is a movement of people campaigning to get rid of nuclear weapons in Britain and worldwide.
Source: www.cnduk.org

Countryside Alliance: is a British organisation promoting issues relating to the countryside.
Source: https://www.countryside-alliance.org

Covid-19: Coronavirus disease is an infectious disease caused by the SARS-CoV-2 virus.
Source: www.who.int/health-topics/coronavirus

CPN: a Community Psychiatric Nurse works with hospitals and visit clients in their own homes, out-patient departments or GP surgeries.
Source: www.rcpsych.ac.uk/mental-health/treatments-and-wellbeing/mental-health-services-and-teams-in-the-community

CSV: UK-wide volunteering charity Community Service Volunteers, commonly known as CSV.
Source: https://volunteeringmatters.org.uk/news/national-charity-community-service-volunteers-csv-becomes-volunteering-matters

Dafydd Thomas: is one of the main characters of the Little Britain franchise portrayed by comedian Matt Lucas.
Source: https://littlebritain.fandom.com/wiki/Daffyd_Thomas

Dante: Inferno is the first part of Italian writer Dante Alighieri's 14th-century epic poem the Divine Comedy.
Source: https://en.wikipedia.org/wiki/Inferno_(Dante)

Dirty Sanchez: is a Welsh stunt and prank TV series featuring a group of three Welshmen and one Englishman harming themselves and each other.
Source: https://dbpedia.org/page/Dirty_Sanchez _(TV_series)

Dr Snuggles: an animated children's television series created by Jeffrey O'Kelly, based on original artwork by Nick Price about a friendly and optimistic inventor who has unusual adventures with his friends.
Source: https://en.wikipedia.org/wiki/Doctor_Snuggles

Dysthymia/Persistent Depressive Disorder (PDD): a long-lasting form of depression which may also have bouts of major depression at times.

There is no clear cause of this disorder, but mental health professionals suggest that certain types of depression seem to run in families - no genes studies have yet been linked.
Source: www.hopkinsmedicine.org/health/ conditions-and-diseases/dysthymia

Elton John: Tantrums & Tiaras is a documentary film about the composer and performing artist Elton John.
Source: https://www.imdb.com/title/ tt0124158

Elvis Presley: American popular singer widely known as the "King of Rock and Roll" and one of rock music's dominant performers from the mid-1950's until his death.
Source: https://www.britannica.com/ biography/Elvis-Presley

Emperor Palpatine: Darth Sidious (born Sheev Palpatine) and also known simply as the Emperor was a human male Dark Lord of the Sith and Emperor of the Galactic Empire, ruling from 19 BBY to 4 ABY.
Source: https://starwars.fandom.com/wiki/ Darth_Sidious

Fellowship Of The Ring: The Fellowship of the Ring is the first of three volumes of the epic novel The Lord of the Rings by the English author J. R. R. Tolkien.
Source: https://en.wikipedia.org/wiki/ The_Fellowship_of_the_Ring

Fortnite: is an online video game developed by Epic Games and released in 2017.
Source: https://www.fortnite.com

Four Seasons: is an international luxury hotel and resort company.
Source: www.fourseasons.com

Gentleman Jack: set in the 1830's in Yorkshire, it stars Suranne Jones as landowner and industrialist Anne Lister.
Source: https://en.wikipedia.org/wiki/ Gentleman_Jack_(TV_series)

Gideon's Bible: holy book distributed by a body of believers dedicated to making the Word of God available to everyone and, together with the local church, reaching souls for Christ.
Source: gideonsinternational.org.uk

Gilligan's Eye: is the sense of optimism from the main protagonist in the American sitcom Gilligan's Island.
Source: https://www.imdb.com/title/tt0057751

Gollum: is a fictional character in J.R.R. Tolkien's Middle-earth legendarium.
Source: https://lotr.fandom.com/wiki/Gollum

Gondor: Gondor was the most prominent kingdom of Men in Middle-earth, bordered by Rohan to the north, Harad to the south, the cape of Andrast and the Sea to the west, and Mordor to the east.
Source: https://lotr.fandom.com/wiki/Gondor

Goon Show: a British radio comedy programme originally produced and broadcast by the BBC Home Service from 1951 to 1960.
Source: https://en.wikipedia.org/wiki/The_Goon_Show

Green Mile: is the tragic story of John Coffey, a gentle giant inmate condemned to death.
Source: https://www.fantasticfiction.com/k/ stephen- king/green-mile.htm

Gregorian Chant: is a form of sacred song in Latin (and occasionally Greek), employed within the Roman Catholic Church for centuries.
Source: https://www.classical-music.com/features/musical-terms/what-is-gregorian-chant

Guardian: a news service owned by Guardian Media Group, which has only one shareholder - the Scott Trust.
Source: www.theguardian.com/uk

Guinness World Records: a site with ultimate record-breaking facts & achievements.
Source: www.guinnessworldrecords.com

Gulf War: was an armed campaign waged by a 39-country military coalition in response to the Iraqi invasion of Kuwait.
Source: https://en.wikipedia.org/wiki/ Gulf_War

Gutenburg Bible: the Gutenberg Bible helped introduce printing to the West, the process was already well-established in other parts of the world.
Source: https://www.history.com/news/7-things-you-may-not-know-about-the-gutenberg-bible

Hand Of God: La mano de Dios was a handling goal scored by Argentine footballer Diego Maradona during the Argentina v England quarter finals match of the 1986 FIFA World Cup.
Source: https://en.wikipedia.org/wiki/The_hand_of_God

Harry Potter: is a series of seven fantasy novels written by British author J.K. Rowling. The novels chronicle the lives of a young wizard and his friends Hermione Granger and Ron Weasley who are students at Hogwarts School of Witchcraft and Wizardry.
Source: https://en.wikipedia.org/wiki/Harry_Potter

Healthy Minds: is an independent user-led mental health charity, providing a range of services for local people to support their wellbeing.
Source: https://www.healthymindscalderdale. co.uk

He-Man: Prince Adam, known as his alter-ego He-Man is a superhero and the main protagonist of the Masters of the Universe franchise.
Source: https://en.wikipedia.org/wiki/He-Man

Hitchhiker's Guide To The Galaxy: Marvin is a robot from the Douglas Adam's science fiction book series. He suffers from Major Depressive Disorder and is a prototype of GPP (Genuine People Personality) and is often referred to as a paranoid android.
Source: www.hero.fandom.com/wiki/ Marvin_the_Paranoid_Android

HRT: patches are used for Hormone Replacement Therapy (HRT) for oestrogen deficiency symptoms in peri- and post-menopausal women.
Source: www.privatedoc.com/medication/ evorel-patches

Hundred Reasons: are an English alternative rock band from Aldershot, Hampshire and Teddington, South West London, formed in 1999.
Source: https://en.wikipedia.org/wiki/Hundred_Reasons

IAPT: Improving Access to Psychological Therapies that helps people to get quick and easy access to the best type of therapy for their individual needs.
Source: www.southwestyorkshire.nhs.uk/services/improving-access-to-psychological-therapies-iapt

Il Buono, Il Brutto, Il Cattivo: a professional gunslinger, a hitman and a wanted outlaw all vying for $200,000.00 worth of gold.
Source: https://www.imdb.com/title/tt0060196

Interpol: the International Criminal Police Organization commonly known as Interpol.
Source: https://www.interpol.int/en

J.K. Rowling: is a British author and creator of the popular and critically acclaimed Harry Potter series.
Source: https://www.britannica.com/ biography/J-K-Rowling

Johnny Cash: is one of the most important, influential and respected artists in the history of recorded music.
Source: https://www.johnnycash.com

Kid Galahad: is a 1962 American musical film starring Elvis Presley as a boxer.
Source: https://en.wikipedia.org/ wiki/Kid_Galahad

Leatherface: Bubba Sawyer is a fictional character and the main antagonist in The Texas Chainsaw Massacre.
Source: https://texaschainsawmassacre. fandom.com/wiki/Leatherface/Original_ Timeline

Liberia: Liberia is a country in West Africa, bordering Sierra Leone, Guinea and Côte d'Ivoire.
Source: https://en.wikipedia.org/wiki/Liberia

Lion's Breath: is a form of pranayama, a breathing exercise from the yogic tradition.
Source: https://www.mindbodygreen.com/ articles/lions-breath

LL Cool J: short for Ladies Love Cool James is an American rapper, songwriter, record producer and actor.
Source: https://en.wikipedia.org/wiki/ LL_Cool_J

Lord Of The Ring-piece: a pornographic spoof of the popular fantasy books and movies - not to be confused with the Scottish podcast or audio drama 'Lords Of The Ring Piece'.
Source: https://www.google.co.uk/ search?q=lord+of+the+ringpiece

Malcolm In The Middle: a show starring Frankie Muniz as Malcolm, the third of four (later five) boys, his brothers and their parents Lois and Hal.
Source: https://malcolminthemiddle.fandom .com/wiki/Malcolm_in_the_Middle

Maslow: Maslow's hierarchy of needs is a motivational theory in psychology comprising a five-tier model of human needs, often depicted as hierarchical levels within a pyramid.
Source: https://simplypsychology.org/maslow.html

Mathew Priest: is an English musician and writer, best known as the drummer for Dodgy, a British pop-rock band who rose to prominence during the 1990s.
Source: https://en.wikipedia.org/wiki/Mathew_Priest

Mental Health Act (Section 2): a law that applies to England and Wales which allows people to be detained in hospital (sectioned) if they have a mental health disorder. You can be detained if:-

- you have a mental disorder

- you need to be detained for a short time for assessment and possibly medical treatment

- it is necessary for your own health or safety or for the protection of other people

The section lasts for up to 28 days, but you may be assessed before the end of the 28 days to see if detainment under a Section 3 is needed.
Source: www.mind.org/mha/section-2

Metuzar: the Eye of the Idol was a wish-granting stone, stolen from the idol of the god Metuzar.
Source: https://gilligan.fandom.com/wiki/Eye_of_the_Idol

Michael Peterson: better known as Charles Bronson, is a British criminal with a violent and notorious life as a prisoner.
Source: https://en.wikipedia.org/wiki/Charles_Bronson_(prisoner)

Michael Winslow: an American actor, comedian and beatboxer billed as The Man of 10,000 Sound Effects for his ability to make realistic sounds using only his voice.
Source: https://en.wikipedia.org/wiki/Michael_Winslow

Mirtazapine: is an atypical antidepressant and is used primarily for the treatment of a major depressive disorder. It can be used for insomnia, panic disorder, post-traumatic stress disorder, obsessive-compulsive disorder, generalized anxiety disorder, social anxiety disorder, headaches, and migraines.
Source: www.ncbi.nlm.nih.gov/books/ NBK519059

Monty Don: is a British horticulturist, broadcaster, and writer who is best known as the lead presenter of the BBC gardening television series Gardeners' World.
Source: https://en.wikipedia.org/wiki/ Monty_Don

Mr. Stink: novel for children from David Walliams; beautifully illustrated by Quentin Blake.
Source: https://shop.scholastic.co.uk/ products/Mr-Stink-David-Walliams- 9780007279067

Mudblood: was a highly derogatory term for either a Muggle or a Muggle-born or half-blood wizard or witch in J.K. Rowling's Harry Potter series.
Source: https://harrypotter.fandom.com/wiki/Mudblood

Nick Heyward: is an English singer-songwriter and guitarist formerly of pop group Haircut One Hundred.
Source: https://nickheyward.com

One Flew Over the Cuckoo's Nest: is a 1975 American psychological comedy drama film directed by Miloš Forman, based on the 1962 novel of the same name by Ken Kesey.
Source: https://en.wikipedia.org/wiki/One_Flew_Over_the_Cuckoo%27s_Nest_(film)

Only Fools And Horses: Uncle Albert was a fictional character in the BBC sitcom Only Fools and Horses portrayed by Buster Merryfield.
Source: https://onlyfoolsandhorses.fandom.com/wiki/Uncle_Albert_Trotter

Open All Hours: classic shop sitcom about miserly shopkeeper Arkwright and his downtrodden nephew and assistant, Granville.
Source: https://www.bbc.co.uk/programmes/ b007h8hp

Pam & Tommy: a stolen VHS tape of the couple on honeymoon in 1995 became the internet's first viral sex video.
Source: https://www.menshealth.com/ entertainment/a38914836/pamela-anderson-tommy-lee-sex-tape-true-story

Paracetamol: Paracetamol belongs to a group of medicines known as analgesics, or painkillers. Paracetamol is used to relieve mild to moderate pain.
Source: https://patient.info/medicine/ paracetamol-calpol-disprol-hedex-panadol

Paradise Lost: an English gothic metal band that formed in 1988 in Halifax, West Yorkshire.
Source: https://en.wikipedia.org/wiki/ Paradise_Lost_(band)

Peddars Way: a 50-mile cycle trail between Thetford and Holme-next-the-Sea.
Source: https://www.nationaltrail.co.uk/ en_GB/short-routes/peddars-way-cycling-route-2

Percy Thrower: was a household name during his long career in gardening programmes on radio and television.
Source: www.thegardenstrust.blog/2015/ 02/07/percy-the-nations-head-gardener

PTSD: Post traumatic Stress Disorder (PTSD & C-PTSD) can affect anyone who has been exposed to trauma – an event or events which provoked fear, helplessness, or horror in response to the threat of injury or death.
Source: www.ptsduk.org

Pulp Fiction: Jules Winfield is a hitman in the Quentin Tarantino movie Pulp Fiction.
Source: https://quentin-tarantino.fandom. com/wiki/Jules_Winnfield

Quetiapine: is used to treat certain mental/mood conditions such as schizophrenia, bipolar disorder, sudden episodes of mania or depression associated with bipolar disorder.

Quetiapine is known as an anti-psychotic drug (atypical type) it works by helping to restore the balance of certain natural substances (neurotransmitters) in the brain.
Source: www.webmd.com/drugs/2/drug-4689-8274/quetiapine-oral/quetiapine-oral/details

Reading Festival: is an annual music festival that takes place in Reading and Leeds, England.
Source: https://www.readingfestival.com/history/reading-1998/

Red Dead Redemption: Red Dead Redemption is a Western-themed action-adventure game played from a third-person perspective.
Source: https://www.rockstargames.com/reddeadredemption

Reginald Perrin: The Fall and Rise of Reginald Perrin is a British sitcom starring Leonard Rossiter in the title role. It is based on a series of novels written by David Nobbs and produced from 1976 to 1979.
Source: https://en.wikipedia.org/wiki/ The_Fall_and_Rise_of_Reginald_Perrin

Reservoir Dogs: Mr. Blonde is a major character in the film Reservoir Dogs, portrayed by Michael Madsen.
Source: https://bloodygta.fandom.com/ wiki/Mr._Blonde

RHS: The Royal Horticultural Society, founded in 1804 as the Horticultural Society of London, is the UK's leading gardening charity.
Source: www.rhs.org.uk

Riders Of Rohan: were the horseback people of Rohan in The Lord Of The Rings trilogy.
Source: https://tolkiengateway.net/wiki / The_Riders_of_Rohan

Ringo Starr: is a British musician, actor, director, writer, and artist best known as the drummer of The Beatles and voice of Thomas The Tank Engine.
Source: www.imdb.com/name/nm0823592

Rita, Sue And Bob Too: a story of working-class Yorkshire life, alternately serious and light-hearted as two schoolgirls have a sexual fling with a married man.
Source: https://www.imdb.com/title/tt0091859

Rockabilly: is an early style of rock and roll music. It dates back to the early 1950s in the United States.
Source: https://en.wikipedia.org/wiki/Rockabilly

Sara Lee: was an American consumer-goods company based in Downers Grove, Illinois.
Source: https://en.wikipedia.org/wiki/Sara_Lee_Corporation

Saturnalia: is an ancient Roman festival and holiday in honour of the god Saturn.
Source: https://www.history.com/topics/ancient-rome/saturnalia

Sertraline: is a type of antidepressant known as a selective serotonin reuptake inhibitor (SSRI). It's often used to treat depression, and also sometimes panic attacks, obsessive compulsive disorder (OCD) and post-traumatic stress disorder (PTSD).
Source: www.nhs.uk/medicines/sertraline/ about-sertraline

Shakin' Stevens: is a Welsh singer and songwriter with four chart-topping hits "This Ole House", "Green Door", "Oh Julie", and "Merry Christmas Everyone".
Source: https://en.wikipedia.org/wiki/ Shakin%27_Stevens

She-Ra: Adora, known by her alter-ego She-Ra is a fictional superheroine in the Masters of the Universe franchise.
Source: https://en.wikipedia.org/wiki/She-Ra

Shibden Hall: is a Grade II listed historic house located in a public park at Shibden, West Yorkshire.
Source: https://museums.calderdale.gov.uk/ visit/shibden-hall

Simon Neil: is a Scottish vocalist, guitarist, and songwriter.
Source: https://www.discogs.com/artist/366661-Simon-Neil

Skippy: the adventures of a young boy and his intelligent pet kangaroo in Waratah National Park, outside Sydney.
Source: www.imdb.com/title/tt0060025

Spaced: a British television sitcom created, written by and starring Simon Pegg and Jessica Stevenson, and directed by Edgar Wright, about the comedic and sometimes farcical misadventures of Daisy Steiner and Tim Bisley.
Source: https://en.wikipedia.org/wiki/Spaced

Split: is a 2016 American psychological thriller starring James McAvoy as the character Kevin Wendell Crumb, a man struggling with dissociative identity disorder (DID).
Source: https://en.wikipedia.org/wiki/Split_(2016_American_film)

Stephen Fry: is an award-winning comedian, actor, presenter and director.
Source: https://www.amazon.co.uk/Stephen-Fry

Sting: a British singer and songwriter known both for being the front man of the band The Police and for his successful solo music and acting career.
Source: www.britannica.com/biography/Sting-British-musician

Stoodley Pike: is a 1,300-foot (400m) hill in the south Pennines noted for the 121-foot (37m) monument at its summit, which dominates the moors of the upper Calder Valley and the market town of Todmorden.
Source: https://en.wikipedia.org/wiki/Stoodley_Pike

Tammy McLeod: set the Guinness World Record for the "fastest time to complete the Hasbro puzzle" with a time of 9 minutes 58.32 seconds in 2020.
Source: https://roomescapeartist.com/2021/05/19/jigsaw-puzzle-world-record-tammy-mcleod

Ten Commandments: a list of rules as recorded in Exodus 20 and Deuteronomy 5.
Source: Moses and or https://lifehopeandtruth.com/bible/10-commandments/the-ten-commandments

Texas Chainsaw Massacre: is a 1974 American horror film produced and directed by Tobe Hooper from a story and screenplay by Hooper and Kim Henkel.
Source: https://en.wikipedia.org/wiki/ The_Texas_Chain_Saw_Massacre

Thelma & Louise: is a 1991 American film directed by Ridley Scott and written by Callie Khouri.
Source: https://en.wikipedia.org/wiki/ Thelma_%26_Louise

Twelve Apostles: stone circle on Burley Moor in Ilkley which comprises of twelve somewhat irregularly spaced stones dating back to the Bronze Age – not to be confused with the Australian Twelve Apostles.
Source: https://yorkshiretimes.co.uk/ article/Twelve-Apostles---Burley-Moor-Ilkley

University Challenge: is a British television quiz programme which first aired in 1962.
Source: https://en.wikipedia.org/wiki/ University_Challenge

Walking Dead: based on the comic book series written by Robert Kirkman, this gritty drama portrays life in the months and years that follow a zombie apocalypse.
Source: https://www.rottentomatoes.com/tv/the_walking_dead

Whamageddon: is a game in which players try to go from 1st December to the end of Christmas Eve without hearing the song "Last Christmas" by Wham!
Source: https://en.wikipedia.org/wiki/Whamageddon

WhatsApp: is an internationally available freeware, cross-platform, centralized instant messaging and voice-over-IP service.
Source: https://www.whatsapp.com

Willy Wonka: Charlie and the Chocolate Factory is a children's book by Roald Dahl, first published in 1964 and features the confectioner Willy Wonka.
Source: https://www.britannica.com/topic/Charlie-and-the-Chocolate-Factory-by-Dahl

Winnie The Pooh: Eeyore is a fictional character in the Winnie-the-Pooh books by A. A. Milne. He is generally characterized as a pessimistic, gloomy, depressed old grey stuffed donkey who is a friend of the title character.
Source: https://en.wikipedia.org/wiki/Eeyore

YouTube: is an American global online video sharing and social media platform
Source: https://www.youtube.com

Zammo: Samuel McGuire was a student at the fictional Grange Hill School from 1982 to 1987, played by Lee MacDonald.
Source: https://grangehill.fandom.com/wiki/Zammo_McGuire

Zig Zag: a stage lighting company established in 1983 as a joint venture by Kev Ludlam and Neil Hunt.
Source: www.zigzaglighting.co.uk

Zopiclone: is used for the short-term (7-14 days) treatment of insomnia in adults and works by binding to a receptor in your brain called the gamma-aminobutyric acid type A (GABAA) receptor and enhancing the action of gamma-aminobutyric acid (GABA), a chemical messenger that has a calming effect.
Source: www.drugs.com/zopiclone.html

Roll Of Honour

Des & Anna, Sarah & Joe, Jim & Mindy, Ceri, Darren (DJi Digi), Geoff & Dee, Helen Taylor, Lesley & Arthur, Gordoooom, Sazza & Dave, The Kerrison's, Bhop & Dori, Matt & Therese, Michelle Haworth, Anne Probets, Lisa Mieszkowska, Tamara, Rachael MacDonald, Pete Foulkes, Martin McIver, Jane Graley, Katie Clark, Danny Lambert, Loz Marklew, Wayne Frear, Justin, Martin, Jamie Robinson, Aaron Stainthorpe, Mark Mason, Tony & Sol Wright and of course Doodles.

Roll Of Dishonour
(the list would be longer than the honour roll)

If you've searched for your name in the credits and it's not there, then you are probably one of those people who looked the other way and didn't want to get involved - all I needed was a "Hey, how are you?"

Disclaimers

* Every effort has been made to protect the characters herein from discredit, hatred, ridicule or contempt which may cause them to be shunned, avoided or lowered in the eyes of society. The names, locations and current whereabouts of individuals have been changed to detract from any libel or defamation claims that may arise and the events portrayed are truthful and accurate to the best of my knowledge.

I am however certifiably bonkers and cannot legally be held responsible for non-compos mentis ramblings, that may have been solicited under medication or periods of clinical depression.

Should any offence be caused to an individual(s) then I am more than happy to elicit a retraction, publicly or otherwise... but let's be honest - it will only be Karen and Len that might be bothered and maybe Lars for merely mentioning a song by his band without first signing in blood.

In any case, anyone mutually associated with us already knows who Karen and Len really are and of the details surrounding our separation and so there's nothing they can claim, that people were not already aware of prior to this publication. Anyone else i.e. the general public, would be using guesswork and I have not disclosed any details that would specifically pin-point the names and addresses of individuals to constitute a disclosure of personal information.

However, should they feel the need to take me to court despite their track records as fabricators of the truth, then I am willing to pay fifty pence per week until I die out of my Universal Credit, or whatever pittance it is that I'm eligible for nowadays.

* Duracell do not promote the ingestion of their products – other brands are available, all of which dissuade self-harm.

* Stephen Fry is a self-confessed teller of untruths as declared in the Fry Chronicles (2010).

* The individual referenced as 'Ringo' is in no way representative of the performer Ringo Starr of The Beatles and is merely based on the metronomic timing of a drummer and the title of a song.

* Richmond Blue have a wide and varied clientele and the characters described in this book are merely a small minority of their customers.

* Latvia is a very nice place and is not full of loons – I merely encountered one that just happened to be from there.

* Rizla do not condone any form of paper cut aggression whilst using their product.

* Sam Smith has clearly demonstrated his flamboyance at the 2023 Brit Awards with his Bowie inspired outfit and identifies as a non-binary gender individual.

* The individual referenced as 'Johnny Bloody Marr' is in no way representative of the amazingly talented performer Johnny Marr of The Smiths and is merely based on the repertoire of the patient.

* Pizza Hut continue to donate pizzas, cash etc. and very proudly support the Mental Health UK charity.

* Morrissey's political leanings are purely based on research of his comments in articles and by his own statements in the media.

* Rockstar Games do not condone any form of violence whilst using the physical versions of their products.

* The individual referenced as 'Harry fucking Secombe' in Songs Of Craze is in no way representative of the late Sir Harry Secombe or the programme Songs Of Praise and is merely based on the choice of singing style of the patient.

* The author is not a medical professional and the content contained herein are personal views and opinions – always read the label and seek medical advice.

Up to £1.00
RAMONES
VOICE OF THE BEEHIVE
RIO ROKZ
STONE SOUR
THE WONDER STUFF
KREATOR
QUEENS HALL
LEEDS
LOVERBOY
L.U.U. ENTS.
LEEDS UNIVERSITY UNION
REFECTORY
NAPALM DEATH
first call
R.E.M.
ROCK CITY
Food

FAITH NO MOR
TERRORVISION
BELLE CHASE HOTEL
DAVIDA
BACKSTAGE
HENRY ROLLINS
University of Bradford Union
Bar
token
NEPHILIM
MILTON KEYNES BOWL
THE RAMONES
IN CONCERT
+ SPECIAL GUESTS
o2 academy
ALICE IN CHAINS
O2 ACADEMY LEEDS
Black Sabbath
Ozzy Osbourne